PIERRE GAGNAIRE
REINVENTING FRENCH CUISINE

PIERRE GAGNAIRE

REINVENTING FRENCH CUISINE

TEXTS BY JEAN-FRANÇOIS ABERT
PHOTOGRAPHS BY PETER LIPPMANN
STYLING AND RECIPE EDITING BY ÉRIC TROCHON
TRANSLATED FROM THE FRENCH BY ANTHONY ROBERTS

STEWART, TABORI & CHANG, NEW YORK

PREFACE

In spite of my persistent and complete allergy to carefully weighted, well-expressed, and clearly articulated recipes, after forty years of cooking I feel it is time to take stock.

My apprenticeship in the profession began on August 23, 1966. I was on holiday in Wimereux, in the north of France, where the colors are soft and filmy, almost humid, like those in the photographs by Peter Lippmann that illustrate this book. A sudden telephone call changed my carefree existence forever. "Come right now, we need an apprentice." The job my father had wanted for me so badly was available. And here I am forty years later.

My years of cuisine have structured me, given me an appetite for a job well done and an enthusiasm for other people, too. My attempts at excellence have led me into much turbulence, doubt, and anxiety; but they have also brought me peace. They have taught me how to speak out, how to love and be loved. Despite all the naysayers, the errors and the catastrophes, to have gotten through these years and earned a modicum of sincere and loyal recognition gives me huge satisfaction, both for myself and for all those on my team who have stayed by my side over the years.

With the rigorous and attentive help of Éric Trochon, I have selected for this book what I consider to be the most significant recipes in the development of my work as a chef since 1966.

In some ways I have come full circle. One of the very first recipes recorded here—an extremely simple one—is for a potato gratin, "seen" more than learned from Monsieur Paul Bocuse in 1965 (Year One for me). The last recipe, just as simple and candid, is a suggestion for haddock that I invented with friends and fellow cooks in mind.

This book does not pretend to be encyclopedic; instead, it is an amazed but clear-eyed look at the forty years of my career, which seem to have passed so quickly. In looking back, I conclude that I'm still at the beginning. My best work is still ahead of me, and that's a promise.

Thank you, Peter, for your openness and rigor, and thank you, Jean-François, for your unwavering friendship. Here's to the dreamers.

—**Pierre Gagnaire**

A man needs time to develop. Pierre Gagnaire didn't always know he'd be a cook and some might say that is precisely why his talent is so unique today. As a young man of insatiable curiosity (even today he remains interested in everything), Pierre fell in love with the plastic arts, jazz, and travel, and like so many others with the same passions his professional future became a matter of increasingly anxious conjecture. To choose a profession, after all, is to commit oneself.

But even the strongest vocations often await the oddest moments to announce themselves. Gagnaire, a keen soccer player, was never at ease with teams that overlooked his potential as an attacker. Now he had to find his own place in the professional world of cuisine, which famously does no one any favors whatsoever.

Pierre had to work under strict constraints during his years of training—and even afterwards, in the family restaurant at Saint-Priest-en-Jarez. He didn't know yet that he would need real freedom before he could realize his full potential in the profession. Nevertheless he accumulated an impressive track record, working with the best in the business, beginning with the great Lyonnais Jean Vignard (who also helped train another soccer-loving chef, Alain Chapel), from whom he learned the fundamentals.

Early Days

I first met Pierre Gagnaire when he was in the final throes of indecision about launching himself heart and soul into the world of haute cuisine. Ever since then we have been close friends. According to Hervé This, whose name will come up again in the pages that follow, a real friendship is for all seasons.

My first meal at the Gagnaire family establishment in Saint-Priest-en-Jarez was worth several cases of Petrus. I concluded that the unknown chef to whom we owed that most joyous of lunches wouldn't be unknown for very long. If he was as good as that, the papers would find him out.

At that time Pierre exuded a wary charm, a tender humility, a fragile sensibility. He was extraordinarily modest about himself. He had an obvious concern for others that was (and remains) most unusual in the world of haute cuisine. The egos of great chefs are seldom in proportion to their true worth; yet at no time has Pierre been remotely narcissistic. What drove him then, as now, was the pleasure his cooking gave to others. You never heard him brag, "I did that really well." More likely he'd remark, "Not bad, right?" pointing at the buttered shellfish he'd just thrown together, as if he himself was removed from it and had slipped, in the blink of an eye, from the role of miracle worker to that of tempted consumer. Later, in his first Saint-Étienne restaurant on the rue Georges-Teissier, his cooking gradually broke free of run-of-the-mill recipes, with taste gaining the upper hand over knowledge. The Gagnaire touch added its own magic to this process. At the time people said there was an element of conjuring about his cooking, as if he could pull rabbits out of his chef's toque.

The Art of Suspense

Today, the idea of Pierre Gagnaire the conjuror has become a cliché. He would be more accurately described as a master of suspense, subtlety, and humor. For example, in a complex entrée made up of six turbulent tableaux called Les Insolites (Oddities), between the delectably mysterious *kokotxas* of hake and the deceptively simple Buren turnip with green tomato juice and silver-tinged olive oil, you will notice an *andouille de Vire* rearing its tumescent head from a nest of little round ratte potatoes. (An equivalently outlandish juxtaposition might be Tintin and his little white dog taking lessons from Roland Barthes.) In today's three-star restaurants, humor is even more rare than cod liver oil. It is all the more delightful in Pierre's case, inasmuch as stuffy, straitlaced gastronomic ritual bans it as ill-bred. Serious gastronomes are like fetishists in their absolute intolerance of the slightest levity about their objects of fantasy, whether these be Breton lobsters or ladies' garters. Each man finds his pleasure where he can and it's nobody's business but his own; still, it will be a sad day when the habitués of Pierre's restaurant on the rue Balzac can no longer spare a smile for the comédie humaine (beginning, of course, with themselves).

Pierre has evolved steadily over the years. His "*insolites*," for example, are like short stories that jauntily traverse a wide diversity of tastes. Recipes of such immaculate precision are actually the stuff of novels. His *canard de Pékin de l'ami Paul*, an homage to Paul Renault, is roasted whole, flavored with a bouillon of herbs flavored ever so faintly with anise, and accompanied by fresh figs and a sublime rosette of *agria* potatoes and dates. It encapsulates in a single dish the three elements of water, earth, and fire—in the manner of the late lamented Chen in his Soleil de l'Est restaurant.

It is not so much that Pierre Gagnaire goes foraging for recipes in distant lands, but rather that, when confronted by all the world's cuisine, he applies to his ideas the supreme refinement of Japanese *iki*. It is a question of distance. He knows how to place himself exactly right: not so far off as to appear indifferent, yet not so close as to seem vulgar. *Iki*, it appears to me, applies to things of the mind and body, as well as to our essential being.

The fact that Pierre can set up a menu like "*les insolites*" followed by his own *canard de Pékin* shows exactly how far he has come. The playful glamour and effervescent color of his creations cannot conceal the fundamental rigor of their design. From the multiple to the unique, from the first dilettantish, delicate flavors of the "*insolites*" to the intensity of the course that follows it, the sequence is perfect. His is the art of blending and dissolving—a limpid expression of the order that a good menu demands, wherein generosity takes precedence over rigor and playfulness over lucidity.

The Cook and the Chemist

In the world of the kitchen, as in the world of the painter, the palette is never entirely set. One can always add to it some fresh nuance of blue, or some unexpected line in sepia. It is in this arena that a new character enters the scene: an intelligent chemist, a scientist who is also a lover of good food. Hervé This has been largely misunderstood, and has even been accused of exerting a malign influence on cooking with his test tubes and powders. Pierre's association with Hervé has been criticized, as if paying attention to molecules somehow marred the imagination of a true cook. The simplest explanation has been overlooked: theirs is a relationship of pure friendship, hence completely disinterested. It may be that from time to time, in a way that could be called pointillist, the chemist brings a note of color to the cook, just as Chevreul once did for the Impressionists. Beyond this, as This puts it, "Cooks have no need of chemists, and chemists have no need of cooks." In any event, from the very start Pierre Gagnaire's way has always led him in the direction of greater liberty and greater clarity, with the Bunsen burner only occasionally assisting the process. With Pierre, there can be no doubt that the arts of the table have entered new realms.

—**Jean-François Abert**

P.S. The recipes in this book span forty years of Pierre Gagnaire's cuisine. The texts that accompany them are divided into three parts: memories shared with him over the years since 1977; food anecdotes, occasionally humorous; and whatever else, given the way Pierre's career has proceeded to date, that might indicate what is yet to come.

CONTENTS

LYON–PARIS, ETC.
LE CLOS FLEURI
SAINT-PRIEST-EN-JAREZ

1 9 6 6

1 9 8 1

Jazz in a Hailstorm

The Roman theater at Vienne is one of the great concert venues in France. In July, between jazz groups, you can see "the night rise," as Victor Hugo put it. You can't quite decide if the stage is inhabited by music or birdsong: the loveliest choruses here have something of a hymn about them, verging on the hypnotic, as though this were the last refuge of serenity in the world. The only problem is that even Roman theaters are vulnerable to the weather, which can make for difficulty in the audience.

A jazz lover from head to toe, Pierre Gagnaire is an habitué of the theater at Vienne. One night there were a couple of musicians on stage—Carla Bley and Steve Swallow—who were also considerable gourmets and admirers of Pierre. Bley's orchestra was at the top of the bill, with Charlie Haden's quartet to follow.

Pierre came to the theater with a few friends. To sharpen their auditory faculties, he had brought along a stack of pigs' ears, some wedges of foie gras clamped between slices of bread, and a bottle of Burgundy from Coche-Dury to quench any immediate thirst. Their neighbors on the benches—whose fare consisted of hot dogs and stale chips—began to quiver with envy. Result: Pierre's food began to ripple outward from him in widening circles. Music is synonymous with conviviality, especially in the summer—some people have even suggested that jazz itself is a seasonal product, like melons, come rain or come shine.

But rain it was that came that night in Vienne, with thunder far louder than trumpets or trombones. It turned Pierre's pigs' ears to jelly, for the Roman theater has no roof, unlike Lasserre or the Tour d'Argent. Everyone was soaked to the skin. But the worst was yet to come. The downpour was followed by hailstones the size of hens' eggs. Many spectators were bruised and cut, and some had to be rushed to the hospital, where they received multiple stitches for their devotion to jazz; their cars were battered to bits outside. But in the fine old tradition of the festival, the show went on; the musicians, who were under cover, continued to play. When the concert came to an end, Pierre and his friends were still there to applaud the Californian Charlie Haden (a respected fellow gourmet, despite the fact that he no longer drinks wine).

Haden looked numb, like a Christian who'd just faced a pride of hungry lions under the eye of Caligula. "Is the weather always this fucking awful?" he inquired. Somebody—I think it was Pierre—was ready with the answer. "Only when you play, Charlie."

J.–F. A.

1965

"LA MARTA"
MY FAVORITES AS A CHILD...

2¹/₄ POUNDS CHOCOLATE (DARK, MILK, OR WHITE)

¹/₂ CUP COCOA BUTTER (OR 10 PERCENT OF THE QUANTITY OF CHOCOLATE USED)

Take a strip of aluminum foil 4 inches wide and cut it into three squares. Fold each square around a wine cork, roll with the flat of your hand on a flat surface, remove the corks, and place the resultant molds on a baking sheet.

Melt 1²/₃ pounds of chocolate in a stainless steel bowl. When the heat reaches 98.6°F (body temperature, i.e. the same as your finger), add the remainder of the chocolate, finely grated. Leave for 3 minutes, then stir with a spatula until the chocolate is smooth.

Dip the foil molds three-quarters of the way into the hot chocolate, then lay them out one by one on a baking sheet covered with wax paper. Place the Martas in a cool place until the chocolate is dry, then carefully peel out the foil, leaving the small chocolate shells intact. They can be filled later with delicate sweet mixtures, at your discretion. Here are some suggestions:

Dark chocolate shells:	candied fruit with crushed almonds, kirsch, orange marmalade
Milk chocolate shells:	fudge, almond paste, fresh almonds
White chocolate shells:	red currant jelly, passion fruit seeds

POTATO GRATIN

Rub the inside of a gratin dish with a peeled garlic clove and coat with fresh butter. Layer the potatoes, cut in thin slices, in the dish, adding salt and pepper to taste. Cover with heavy cream and bake in a preheated oven (350°F) until the potatoes are golden and all the cream has been absorbed.

THE WHOLE ART OF THE GRATIN LIES IN GAUGING CORRECTLY THE DIMENSIONS
OF THE DISH AND THE THICKNESS OF THE LAYER OF POTATOES. THE POTATOES
SHOULD NEVER BE MORE THAN 1¼ INCHES DEEP.

1966

TERRINE DE LIÈVRE (HARE TERRINE)
CHEZ JEAN VIGNARD

Serves 4

1 HARE (3¹/₈ POUNDS OF MEAT)

HARE STOCK
1 TABLESPOON OIL
4 TEASPOONS UNSALTED BUTTER
1 WHITE ONION, DICED
1 CARROT, DICED
2¹/₈ CUPS WATER
BOUQUET OF BAY LEAF, THYME, AND
ROSEMARY

HARE STUFFING
1¹/₄–1¹/₂ POUNDS RAW FOIE GRAS
2¹/₄ POUNDS FAT PORK NECK, SLICED INTO
SMALL CUBES
1 POUND MINCED LEAN PORK NECK
3/4 POUND DUCK OR CHICKEN LIVERS
(DUCK LIVERS ARE BEST)
1/2 POUND HARE'S LIVER
4 EGGS
1/2 CUP FINELY CHOPPED TRUFFLE
3¹/₂ TABLESPOONS TRUFFLE JUICE
1/3 CUP PORT
3/4 CUP *MARC DE BOURGOGNE*
3/4 CUP REDUCED HARE STOCK
2¹/₂ TABLESPOONS SALT
FRESHLY GROUND PEPPER
1 STRIP FRESH PORK BELLY

Debone the hare (reserve the bones) and trim, removing the tendons. Cut the meat into large cubes. Set aside.

HARE STOCK

Crush the bones and roast them in the oil and a pat of butter. When they are well roasted, discard the fat and replace it with the remaining butter. Add the onion and the carrot, brown, and cover with water. Add the herb bouquet and simmer for 1 hour. Strain the stock through a fine-mesh sieve and reduce by three-quarters until syrupy. Set aside at room temperature.a

HARE STUFFING (PREPARE 36 HOURS IN ADVANCE)

Chop the foie gras into large cubes the same size as the cubes of hare meat. Chop the pork neck (lean and fat together) into smaller cubes. Pass the duck or chicken livers with the hare liver through a meat grinder.
Mix all these ingredients in a large bowl, add the eggs one by one, stirring in the truffle, truffle juice, port, *marc,* hare stock, freshly ground pepper, and salt as you go. Take special care not to break up the foie gras.
Press into a terrine lined with thin strips of pork belly and refrigerate for 36 hours.
Cover the terrine with foil or a fitted lid and cook in a bain-marie for about 1¹/₂ hours in an oven preheated to 350°F. Set aside to cool.
If you can store the terrine in the refrigerator for a week before serving, you'll find it even more delicious.

A RECIPE INCLUDED IN HOMAGE TO ALAIN CHAPEL—JEAN VIGNARD'S APPRENTICE
TWENTY YEARS BEFORE ME—AT WHOSE RESTAURANT I FIRST TASTED THIS SENSATIONAL
TERRINE. A PARTICULAR JOY OF PÂTÉS AND TERRINES IS THEIR PRESENCE ON THE TABLE
SURROUNDED BY SPECIAL CONDIMENTS LIKE GHERKINS, PICKLES, AND TINY
VINEGARY ONIONS. TODAY I WOULD ADD PICKLED CHANTERELLES,
QUINCE MARMALADE, AND APPLES PURÉED WITH PINE NUTS.

POULET AU VINAIGRE
CHEZ JEAN VIGNARD

First, prepare the sauce base: Whisk together the mustard, tomato paste, and white wine. Set aside.

Heat the oil in a heavy-bottomed casserole and brown the chicken pieces with the garlic and butter. When they are golden, remove some of the cooking fat and deglaze with 2 tablespoons of vinegar (one white, one red). Cover the casserole, reduce the heat, and cook for another few minutes. Turn the pieces of chicken over, add a little more vinegar, and cover again. Repeat this process four or five times.

By now each piece of chicken should be caramelized. Continue cooking, taking great care not to burn the chicken. Add the reserved sauce base, cover, and bring to a boil. Allow to simmer very gently for 10–12 minutes. Remove the pieces of chicken, place them on a serving platter, and keep warm. Discard the garlic and strain the sauce through a fine-mesh sieve into a small saucepan. Add the cream little by little, and correct the seasoning.

BEFORE SERVING

Nap the pieces of chicken with the sauce. Serve with white rice or pilaf.

Serves 4

ONE 3$^1/_2$-POUND CHICKEN, CUT IN PIECES

4 TABLESPOONS STRONG MUSTARD

3 TABLESPOONS TOMATO PASTE

1 CUP PLUS 1 TABLESPOON DRY WHITE WINE

2 UNPEELED GARLIC CLOVES

6$^1/_2$ TABLESPOONS UNSALTED BUTTER

$^2/_3$ CUP WHITE WINE VINEGAR

$^2/_3$ CUP RED WINE VINEGAR

3$^1/_2$ TABLESPOONS OIL

3$^1/_2$ TABLESPOONS HEAVY CREAM

SALT AND PEPPER

THIS DISH IS AN ABSOLUTE STANDARD, PREPARED WITH THE SIMPLEST OF INGREDIENTS.
POULET DE BRESSE RISSOLÉ, TOMATE ET VINAIGRE WAS ALL THE RAGE IN LYON
DURING THE 1960S—WE COULDN'T GET ENOUGH OF IT.

La Tante in Decline

Quenelles de brochet like canal barges, breasting rivers of cream. Dover sole gleaming in sunbursts of butter. Hors d'oeuvres like they used to be, with names like *clapotons, dents de Lyon, gras-double en salade*; heavyweight dishes to match the heavy-bottomed *pots de Beaujolais* of local tradition. That was Tante Alice, once upon a time.

Indeed, this was what everything used to be like in Lyon, a city that cherished its image for hearty eating. At that time, the mere sight of the Lyon railway station, the Gare de Perrache, gave the novelist Julien Gracq an overwhelming urge to hang himself. What remained of the city's pride was to be found in its red wine sauces—*miroirs*, they were called—which mostly reflected the local casseroles (culinary and judicial) and stews (political). The citizens of Lyon seemed to withdraw into holes in the wall that they called *bouchons*. People from other parts of France allowed that those in Lyon still had a talent for soups—and, once a year, would visit them in their soup-and-Beaujolais museums, where they found them as interesting as dioramas.

In those days the restaurants of Lyon were stacked with more trophies than dinner plates. The Lyon soccer team, Olympique Lyonnais, was still on a pedestal. There was a restaurant on the Presqu'île that offered classic and thoroughly authentic local cuisine; its clientele was all the more devoted because the prices were reasonable. The place was called Tante Alice (in the tradition of La Mère Brazier or La Mère Jean), and three of the twentieth century's most famous chefs worked there at one time or another: Alain Chapel, Bernard Pacaud, and Pierre Gagnaire. Not bad for a neighborhood restaurant.

Before I go any further, I should describe the kind of place it was. Between 1960 and 1970 the rue des Remparts d'Ainay, between the Saône and Rhone rivers, had a reputation as a thoroughly bourgeois preserve. Alighting there between trains, journalists from Paris would mutter clichés about the double lives of the Lyonnais middle class—frequenters of church in the morning and brothels at night. Although the clichés were about as substantial as *soupe à l'oignon*, the nice thing about clichés is that people never get enough of them, even when you dish them out with a ladle.

If one took a closer at the rue des Remparts d'Ainay back then, it revealed itself as a street whose inhabitants were gently aging, generally petit bourgeois, right-thinking, and about as wicked as a parish newsletter. The brothels had retired, with dignity, to the other side of the Place Bellecour or closer to the Saône. Meanwhile, the city's grands bourgeois had settled on the left bank of the river for good. A few shops remained in the shadow of the Abbaye d'Ainay, along with a bookbindery, some honorable elderly ladies who restored lampshades in the back of a dark shop, and a *crémière* who filled milk churns in the old-fashioned way and made a wonderful salty butter that my grandmother loved.

It was a less than stimulating environment, and Pierre Gagnaire was thoroughly bored at Tante Alice. His culinary fate at the time was entirely controlled by his father (one can readily imagine Spencer Tracy playing the role of the father at this stage in the story).

My own father took me to eat at Tante Alice on several occasions. Today I sometimes speculate that I might have lunched on a sole prepared by the young Pierre Gagnaire—who knows? Life is full of strange twists of fate, whereby we pass within a hair's breadth of grand passions, epiphanies of all sorts, enduring friendships, and sudden death.

Today the memory of Tante Alice has faded as surely as yesterday's lunch menu chalked on a bistro blackboard. The restaurant still exists, but it has adopted the public demeanor of an anonymous chef, which is about the worst and dreariest thing that can befall a restaurant: To do this, as Cioran would say, is to "tinker with the incurable." The *soles meunières* have fallen asleep. The *quenelles* have floated away, over-laden.

Someday, if you happen to be in the vicinity of the Abbaye d'Ainay, a passerby may ask you the whereabouts of the Tante Alice restaurant, and you may wish to answer that you too would like to know. One thing is certain: Pierre Gagnaire doesn't work in the rue des Remparts d'Ainay anymore.

J.–F. A.

1968

SOLE "TANTE ALICE"
CHEZ TANTE ALICE

Serves 4

2 WHOLE SOLE, 2–2¹/₂ POUNDS EACH

¹/₄ CUP UNSALTED BUTTER

2 FINELY CHOPPED SHALLOTS

1 GLASS WHITE WINE (CHARDONNAY)

1¹/₄ CUPS FISH STOCK (PREFERABLY MADE FROM SOLE)

²/₃ CUP THICK HEAVY CREAM

SALT

Skin each sole on both sides, rinse gently with water, and remove the insides and roes. Pat dry with a paper towel.

Butter an ovenproof baking dish, sprinkle with salt, and spread the chopped shallots over the bottom. Place the soles on top, making sure they lie flat. Add the white wine and the fish stock, cover with buttered wax paper, and cook for 10 minutes in an oven preheated to 350°F.

Remove the baking dish from the oven and set aside for 10 minutes. Then carefully lift away the fillets of sole, setting aside the heads and backbones, and reassemble the fish on a heat-proof serving platter. Keep warm. Return the bones and heads to the cooking liquid and reduce it by three-quarters. Add the cream and reduce again by three-quarters.

Strain the sauce through a *chinois* (a conical, fine-mesh strainer) and correct the seasoning before incorporating the remaining butter. Nap the fish with the sauce.

BEFORE SERVING

Place the fish under the broiler for about 3 minutes to glaze them. Serve immediately.

THIS IS ONE OF THE GREAT CLASSICS OF FRENCH COOKING. I LOVE ITS BEAUTIFUL, BUTTERY-IVORY, UNCTUOUS SAUCE, WHICH LINGERS ON THE TONGUE AND IS NEVER TOO HEAVY. IT'S A DISH THAT EXPRESSES THE SENSITIVITY OF THE PERSON WHO COOKS IT. TODAY I WOULD MAKE IT MORE DISTINCTIVE BY ADDING INGREDIENTS WE DIDN'T KNOW WOULD WORK AT THE TIME: LIKE NOILLY PRAT VERMOUTH OR AN AMONTILLADO SHERRY, OR A TOUCH OF BLOOD ORANGE, OR EVEN SOME GRATED LIME PEEL.

HOMARD "ERNEST RENAN"
CASINO DE CHARBONNIÈRES

Cut the lobster in two lengthwise, remove the meat from body, claws, and joints, and set aside.

Cut the tail meat into medallions. Set aside the best ones, dice the remainder and mix with the meat from the claws and joints (this is for the *salpicon*). Lay the half-shells of the lobster in a deep dish.

Blend the cream and the reduced port in a small casserole, and add the shellfish stock. Bring to a boil and reduce until the sauce is smooth and thick enough to coat a spoon. Add the truffle juice, salt, and cayenne pepper. Set aside the best slices of truffle, finely chop the rest, and stir them into the sauce. Add the lemon juice and the butter little by little, stirring vigorously with a whisk.

Pour the sauce over the medallions of lobster and the *salpicon*. Heat gently over low heat for 5 minutes, while the tastes meld and impregnate the meat.

Place the empty lobster half-shells in an oven preheated to 325°F.

BEFORE SERVING

Lay the *salpicon* along the bottom of each lobster half-shell, and place the medallions of lobster on top, alternating with slices of truffle. Place a claw on each head. Nap generously with sauce and serve immediately.

Serves 2

ONE 1³/₄-POUND COOKED LOBSTER (SEE PAGE 194)

1 SCANT CUP HEAVY CREAM

1²/₃ CUPS FINE PORT, REDUCED BY THREE-QUARTERS

1 SCANT CUP SHELLFISH STOCK

7 TABLESPOONS TRUFFLE JUICE

ONE 1-OUNCE (A GENEROUS OUNCE) TRUFFLE, THICKLY SLICED

SQUEEZE OF LEMON JUICE

2 TEASPOONS UNSALTED BUTTER

SALT

PINCH OF CAYENNE PEPPER

A SUBLIME RECIPE, SIMPLE TO ACCOMPLISH, BUT INVOLVING HIGHLY
SOPHISTICATED INGREDIENTS. THIRTY YEARS AGO IT WAS HARD TO IMAGINE THAT
LOBSTERS COULD REACH US ALIVE. THEY WERE COOKED WAY IN ADVANCE AND KEPT
IN THE COLD ROOM. TODAY, WHEN INSTANT COOKING AND FRESH PRODUCE ARE
SACROSANCT, THIS WOULD BE CONSIDERED LITTLE SHORT OF CRIMINAL.

POMMES MAXIM'S

ONE OF MY FRIENDS DURING MY MILITARY SERVICE WAS A MAN WHO'D WORKED IN THE KITCHEN

AT MAXIM'S, IN PARIS. HE SHOWED ME THIS RECIPE. IF YOU DO POTATOES THIS WAY, THEY TURN OUT

CRISPY, GOLDEN, AND VERY DELICIOUS, WITH A NUTTY TASTE OF BUTTER.

IT WAS A REAL DISCOVERY—DELUXE POTATO CHIPS!

1971

POMMES MAXIM'S
SERVICE MILITAIRE

Peel your potatoes, which should be firm-fleshed, then cut them in $1^1/_4$–$1^1/_2$-inch-diameter cylinders and dry them in a clean kitchen towel. Do not wash them in water, which will leech away some of their starch.

Slice the cylinders of potato finely to a thickness of $1/_{16}$ inch, using a mandoline. Mix the rounds with warm clarified butter, then lay them on a nonstick baking sheet, sprinkle with salt, and cook in a an oven preheated to 400°F. Serve with roast meat or chicken.

BÉCASSE (WOODCOCK)
CHEZ LUCAS CARTON

Pluck the woodcocks very carefully, including the heads. Wrap each bird in a strip of fresh lard (or bacon if you have no lard), wedging the beak between the thighs. Roast the woodcocks in a small pan with a little oil and some butter, cooking them as quickly as possible; be very careful not to burn the lard.

When done, allow to cool for 15 minutes in the fat. Remove the breasts and keep them warm in the fat, and set aside the lard, which should now be crisp.

Rub a little fat on thick slices of bread and place them under the broiler until golden.

Preparing the rôties: Pass the woodcocks' innards through a *tamis* (a fine-mesh, drum sieve), having first removed the gizzards. Mix them with a little mustard, a spoonful of puréed foie gras, and a dash of good brandy. Add pepper—but not too much. Spread the slices of toast with this preparation and garnish with strips of lard.

Now crush the carcasses well, roast them, and press their concentrated juices through a fine-mesh strainer. Split the heads and put them aside, keeping them warm.

Reheat the breasts in a pan, with their fat. Cover the pan, and when the fat begins to sizzle (*chanter*, or "sing," is the charming French word for this), sprinkle them with a little good brandy. Serve the breasts in the same pan.

At the table, with everyone looking on, lay out the breasts on the hot dinner plates side by side with the *rôties* and the split heads.

Finally, pour a few drops of ice-cold water into the pan to loosen the roasting deposits, then add the concentrated woodcock essence and spoon a little of this jus onto the plates next to each breast.

Garnish the woodcocks with Pommes Maxim's (see recipe on facing page) or a crisp salad—such as chicory—with a sharp dressing.

THIS IS MUCH MORE THAN A RECIPE. IT'S ONE OF COOKING'S GREAT JOYS,
ON THE RARE OCCASIONS WHEN ONE CAN OBTAIN THIS WONDERFUL GAME BIRD.
DECIDING HOW LONG WOODCOCK SHOULD HANG BEFORE THEY ARE COOKED
IS A DELICATE AFFAIR. PERSONALLY I DON'T LIKE THEM TOO GAMEY.

1974

SOUFFLÉ MARIE-LOUISE
CHEZ LUCAS CARTON

Serves 4

8 APRICOT HALVES IN SYRUP

1 VANILLA BEAN, SPLIT IN HALF
LENGTHWISE AND SCRAPED

2 TEASPOONS UNSALTED BUTTER

4 TABLESPOONS APRICOT EAU-DE-VIE
(NOYAUX DE POISSY)

1¾ OUNCES GENOISE CAKE, CUT INTO
SMALL DIAMOND SHAPES

1 TABLESPOON POWDERED SUGAR

2 TEASPOONS SOFTENED, UNSALTED
BUTTER FOR THE SOUFFLÉ DISH

1 TABLESPOON SUGAR FOR THE
SOUFFLÉ DISH

SOUFFLÉ MIXTURE

3½ TABLESPOONS ALL-PURPOSE FLOUR

⅔ CUP MILK

⅓ CUP GRANULATED SUGAR PLUS A PINCH
MORE FOR THE WHIPPED EGG WHITES

1 TABLESPOON ALMOND PASTE

1 TEASPOON UNSALTED BUTTER

PINCH OF SALT

3 EGG YOLKS

4 EGG WHITES

Drain the apricots and sauté them with a little butter along with the vanilla bean and seeds. When they are golden, deglaze with apricot eau-de-vie. Set aside at room temperature in a small container.

Prepare a soufflé dish: Paint the soufflé dish with softened butter using a brush, then sprinkle the inside with powdered sugar. Turn the dish over and tap it to remove the excess sugar. Once you have prepared the mold, take particular care not to put your fingers inside, which may cause the soufflé to catch on its sides and not rise straight.

Prepare a bain-marie (double boiler): Pour boiling water into a dish large enough to hold your soufflé dish with room to spare.

Stir together the milk and flour in a pan, add the sugar, and cook the mixture over low heat for about 5 minutes, until it thickens. Remove from the fire, then add the almond paste and butter, followed by the egg yolks. Gently incorporate the egg whites, beaten until stiff with a pinch of sugar.

Pour some of this preparation into a buttered and sugared soufflé dish. Lay the diamonds of genoise cake in the bottom and sprinkle them with apricot liqueur. Cover with the rest of the preparation. Smooth flat, then place the apricot halves, round side up, on top. Place the dish in the bain-marie, allow it to sit for 5 minutes, then bake in an oven preheated to 350°F for 25–30 minutes.

BEFORE SERVING

Sprinkle powdered sugar on the soufflé as soon as it is removed from the oven. Serve immediately.

THIS IS AN INTERESTING CLASSIC, WHICH I HAVE NOT ALTERED.
IT OFTEN HAPPENS THAT COOKS TREAT CLASSICS AS ROUTINE, AND AS A RESULT
THE ORIGINAL RECIPE IS ALLOWED TO GO ADRIFT UNTIL IT BECOMES
QUITE DREARY AND MEDIOCRE. IN COOKING, ALL THE SENSES SHOULD BE
KEPT SHARP—ONE SHOULD BE CONSTANTLY ON GUARD AGAINST DRIFT.

BAR À LA BARIGOULE
BASTIDE DE TOURTOUR

BARIGOULE

Cut the artichoke stems to 2 inches. Remove the leaves using a small, very sharp knife. Halve the hearts, rub them with half a lemon, and brown them in half of the olive oil. When they are golden, add the onion, the carrot, and the diced bacon. Cover and simmer 3 minutes. Then add the white wine and vinegar, along with the herbs, fennel and coriander seeds, and finally the tomato. Add salt and pepper, cover, and let cook gently for about 35 minutes.

When the cooking is done, the sauce will be reduced and the artichokes will be well caramelized. Spoon the *barigoule* into a baking dish.

SEA BASS

Lay the sea bass fillet (seasoned with salt and spread with the remaining oil) on the garnish, and cook in an oven preheated to 400°F for about 10 minutes.

BEFORE SERVING

Place the artichokes on each of four dinner plates and lay the sea bass fillet beside them, on top of the *barigoule.*

Serves 4

4 SEA-BASS FILLETS, SKIN, SCALES, AND BONES REMOVED

BARIGOULE

12 SMALL, YOUNG ARTICHOKES

1/2 LEMON

1 SCANT CUP OLIVE OIL

1 CHOPPED ONION, CUT IN SMALL DICE

1 CARROT, CUT IN SMALL DICE

3/4 CUP SMOKED BACON, CUT IN LARDONS

1 GLASS WHITE WINE

DASH OF WHITE VINEGAR

BOUQUET OF AROMATIC HERBS (THYME, BAY LEAF, ROSEMARY, SAVORY)

PINCH OF FENNEL SEEDS

PINCH OF CORIANDER SEEDS

1 LARGE TOMATO, PEEELED, SEEDED, AND COARSLEY CHOPPED

SALT AND PEPPER

SEA BASS

WITH MY FIRST JOB AS A CHEF CAME MY FIRST ENCOUNTER WITH PROVENCE,

WHERE I DISCOVERED BABY ARTICHOKES, HITHERTO UNKNOWN TO ME,

AND SEA BASS. TOGETHER, THEY MAKE A PERFECT PROVENÇAL MARRIAGE.

EVEN SO, THIS RECIPE BRINGS BACK PAINFUL MEMORIES OF THE TIME

I SERVED A SEA BASS TO THE TROISGROS FAMILY—AND MADE A COMPLETE HASH OF IT.

Gagnaire's "Pochette"

I spent 1977 writing a food guide to the Rhone-Alpes region, a "baroque and fatiguing exercise," as Roger Nimier might have said. People imagine a job like this to be a dream, but it really isn't.

At the time I adored first-rate cooking like Alain Chapel's, but I also liked the convivial *bouchons* of Lyon, provided they were run with humility. And I didn't mind a few hours of honest writing every day. Given that the quality expected of food writers was never very high, my reputation as a writer was not at risk and I was confident I could make the work a pleasure.

I was a young man whose palate was completely naïve and whose writing was even more credulous, but what happened to me subsequently was a grave, unpardonable error. After seven years of guide writing and three decades of food commentary in newspapers, I see that what I accomplished was precisely the reverse: Poor fool that I was, I transformed my greatest pleasure into work.

The final days of research for that first guide were totally exhausting. The deadlines loomed ever nearer in those chilly hotel rooms where I lodged. I assiduously delivered my judgments on *coppas* (avocados stuffed with prawns or crabmeat), which I declared a black crime; and monkfish sorbet, the perpetrators of which I smote fiercely, on behalf of future generations of innocent consumers. Lunch at an auberge was followed inexorably by dinner at a restaurant, and between meals I rinsed my mouth out (metaphorically) with paper.

In September 1977, the work reached a climax as my final deadline loomed only a few days away. On September 4, I booked lunch for my wife, Marie-José, and me at the restaurant of Michel Rostang, who was still at Sassenage at the time (he later moved on to Paris). On the menu was a *pot au feu marinière*, sweetbreads and veal kidneys in red wine, cheeses, *tarte aux mirabelles*, and *tarte au citron*. The wines helped wash all this down, notably a very pleasant Puligny-Montrachet (Les Pucelles '74, made by Vincent Leflaive) and a charming Savigny-les-Beaune (from Tollot-Beart). In the evening we came very close to disqualifying a Grenoble restaurant from the guide: *potage parmentier*, *sole meunière*, two glasses of Macon. In between, we viewed the de Kooning exhibition at the Musée des Beaux Arts; although at first we were rather groggy, de Kooning's wild colors and brushwork set us firmly back on our feet.

On the 5th, we visited a one-star restaurant near Grenoble: *saumon mariné aux herbes du jardin*, *entrecôte au Bouzy*, cheeses, *tarte au café*, chocolate mousse. We drank Bouzy, appropriately, before crashing in the local cinema. Little did we know that September 8, then almost upon us, would be a historic date in our lives.

Neither Marie-José nor I knew a thing about the Clos Fleuri at Saint-Priest-en-Jarez, apart from a few vague rumors of *jambon dans le foin*. We had never heard of Pierre Gagnaire, who at the time was still waiting in the anteroom of *grande cuisine* and probably contemplating a career playing the clarinet or selling spices.

The first surprise was that there was no *jambon dans le foin* on the menu. The second surprise was that our lunch—consumed in the restaurant's garden, under a warm September sun—revealed a joyous riot of flavors. Above all, a dish called *pochette de Saint-Pierre aux poivrons doux* opened up our palates like the first edition of a book we had been looking for all our lives. It was a fairground of aromas and revealed tastes, subtle and never too pungent, demonstrating great artistry. The *pochette* (the French word for a handkerchief worn in the breast pocket) demonstrated far more than the cook's allegiance to old-fashioned elegance. When we looked into that *pochette*, believe me, we could foretell the future of Pierre Gagnaire. We sensed his tenderness in the taste and texture of the sweet peppers; indeed, we believed that this Saint Pierre would receive the keys to whatever paradise the Lord reserves for great cooks.

Reader, knowing you to be insatiable, I will give you the rest of the menu of that memorable day: *noisette d'agneau à l'échalote et à l'ail en chemise*, cheeses, vanilla and pistachio ice cream. Then a chocolate cake, coffee, and the check.

We didn't catch so much as a glimpse of the cook. My friendship with Pierre Gagnaire would blossom a year later, around a *tourte de grenouilles* that he made. But as far as I'm concerned, it started with that first *pochette de Saint-Pierre*.

J.–F. A.

JOHN DORY WITH SWEET PEPPERS
AU CLOS-FLEURI

Serves 4

4 JOHN DORY FILLETS (PORGY CAN BE SUBSTITUTED)

2 SWEET RED BELL PEPPERS

2 SMALL ONIONS

ONE 2–2¹/₂-INCH-LONG EUROPEAN HOTHOUSE CUCUMBER, PEELED (ABOUT ¹/₄ CUP DICED)

4 LEMON SLICES

SALT AND FRESHLY GROUND PEPPER

¹/₄ CUP WHITE WINE

¹/₄ CUP OLIVE OIL

Char the bell peppers over an open flame. When the skin is well blackened, enclose them into a plastic bag and let cool. Scrape the skin off the peppers and rinse under the tap. Drain well on paper towels, then slice into strips and set aside.

Chop the onions into rings and dice the cucumber. Lay four strips of aluminum foil 1 foot long on a work surface. Divide the onion rings equally among the strips, along with the diced cucumber and sliced bell peppers. Lay the fish fillets on the vegetables and top with a slice of lemon. Season with salt and pepper, a spoonful of wine, and a spoonful of oil to each papillote, then seal as tightly as possible by folding and pinching the foil into a secure packet.

Lay the papillotes carefully on a baking sheet and bake in an oven preheated to 400°F for 7 minutes.

BEFORE SERVING

Remove the papillotes from the oven; they should be nicely puffed. Place them on hot dinner plates and bring them to the table as they are. The guests should open their papillotes simultaneously, so everyone can enjoy the wonderful aromas to the maximum.

POCHETTE DE SAINT-PIERRE

THIS WAS THE RECIPE THAT REALLY STARTED IT ALL:

MAXIMUM ECONOMY OF MEANS, NO CALCULATION, AND

NO NOTION OF TIME IN THE COOKING OF FISH.

SUCH WAS JEAN-FRANÇOIS ABERT'S SUCCINCT DESCRIPTION,

AND IT OPENED MY EYES TO THE 'ACT OF COOKING.'

SAINT-ÉTIENNE
RUE GEORGES-TEISSIER

1981

1992

Soccer and Beets

The charm of the countryside around Killarney: melancholy, elegant landscapes, varnished by rain. While riding along in a one-horse shay, visitors to Ireland try to forget that vacation season is drawing to a close. As the Irish proverb has it: "God made time aplenty."

On September 1, 2000, at the other end of the island, the Irish soccer team was due to meet the formidable Netherlands team in the knockout stages of the World Cup. Soccer is not the most important of Ireland's sporting pre-occupations; the Irish prefer their national games of hurling and Gaelic football. In general they play soccer like prudent amateurs. At the time there was a total of about forty-five Irishmen in the professional game of soccer, most of whom played for English clubs; from among these the Eire soccer team was selected. Although drawn from a tiny pool of players, they were not without ardor; as everyone knows, the wearing of the green often inspires an Irishman to mighty deeds. Often in the minority in the past, the Irish have suffered and come through. And forty-five is as good a number as any.

That September day, Pierre Gagnaire was in Killarney with a friend—myself—who kept bending his ear about the fighting Irish. In the center of town was a pub where the match was playing on a giant television screen. To miss a game that was this important to his hosts would be a blasphemy tantamount to booing the "Marseillaise" at the Stade de France.

If you wanted a table reasonably close to the screen, you had to book a couple of hours in advance and resign yourself to lunch in the pub. One had to block out the reek of grease from the kitchen and the scraps coagulating on the floor—the place looked like Francis Bacon's studio, minus the champagne. Anywhere else, in Cork for example, or in Dublin's delicious Chapter One restaurant next to the Writers' Museum, or at Thornton's, Ireland was fully attuned to the pleasures of the table. But here, in the pub in Killarney, all you could get was "plain food," which was actually not plain at all, but cruelly tortured, grill-marked, scorched by out-of-control ovens, and humiliated by sauces that tasted like pelargonium mixed with burned stock cubes. We dutifully flushed all this down our gullets with thick, creamy, bittersweet Guinness.

The match was sublime. The first half was extraordinarily tense, the score nil-nil at the interval. The second half began with sending off one of the Irish players who lost his temper and kicked his adversary. In the pub, the atmosphere grew blacker than Guinness itself. The groans and complaints from the bar grew louder, as if the occasion were no longer a game but another battle of the Boyne, with Dutch William back again to crush the Irishry.

But then a miracle happened, the kind that only occurs in this land of saints. One of the Irish midfielders, Jason McAteer, struck a goal that was completely improbable, but nonetheless unstoppable. The house erupted with patriotic joy. People were roaring, applauding, wrapping each other in bear hugs. Even Pierre Gagnaire momentarily resembled a man who'd never cooked anything but Irish stew. The Irish were ten men against eleven, they won the match by one goal to nil, and it was an exploit to make the rain stop falling in Killarney.

But there comes a moment when even the greatest victories begin to recede into memory, when the heroes of the hour hang up their boots and life returns to its usual tempo. Dusk was falling and the pub food was churning in our bellies. Pierre and his friend withdrew to the Kenmare Park Hotel, to dine among worldly people who cared not a jot for soccer or for Ireland's triumph at the game.

And we felt bereft, missing both France and the Ireland we had just left behind in the pub. We looked for our roots on the menu, and fell upon a dish that included beets, fittingly enough. Pierre had long ago forsaken his trademark beet chips, having seen them copied by too many of his colleagues. No matter that at the Kenmare Park Hotel the vegetable arrived ingenuously wrapped in a slice of smoked salmon, or that the cooking was about as similar to that of the rue Balzac as an ostrich steak might be to an *agneau de pré salé*.

No matter indeed. It had been a joyous day, the sort that calls for a great Margaux. We chose as a substitute a Chateau La Gurgne '85 to go with the entirely forgettable *plat de résistance*, and noted that it had retained some of its original lively spiciness and fruit. A Margaux '82 or '96 would have been better, but *tant pis*.

J.-F. A.

OYSTER JELLY AND DUCK FOIE GRAS

AT SAINT-ÉTIENNE I HAD A SMALL PRODUCER WHO BROUGHT ME

SUPERB BEETS, COOKED ON A WOOD FIRE! CUBES OF BEET, THEIR JUICES REDUCED,

BEAUFORT CHEESE, AND NATURAL OYSTER WATER—

A COMPLETELY UNEXPECTED ENCOUNTER BETWEEN SEA AND LAND.

FOR ME, THE BEET IS THE ONLY VEGETABLE THAT HAS AN AUTHENTIC PERFUME OF IODINE.

1981

SEAFOOD PLATTER

Serves 4

4 LARGE OYSTERS

3 SCALLOPS, VERY THINLY SLICED

SHELLFISH

4 VENUS CLAMS (OR SUBSTITUTE MANILA)

8 COMMON CLAMS (SUCH AS LITTLENECKS)

9 OUNCES COCKLES (WELL SOAKED IN WATER TO RINSE OUT THE SAND)

1 SHALLOT, FINELY CHOPPED

2 TEASPOONS UNSALTED BUTTER

1 GLASS WHITE WINE

12 SMALL SCALLOPS

1 LEEK, WHITE PART ONLY

FOIE GRAS BUTTER

2 OUNCES COOKED FOIE GRAS

1 GLASS WHITE WINE (CHARDONNAY)

2 GRAY SHALLOTS, FINELY CHOPPED

²/₃ CUP UNSALTED BUTTER

SALT AND FRESHLY GROUND PEPPER

DASH OF SHERRY VINEGAR

SHELLFISH

Sweat the shallot in a casserole with the butter, pour in the white wine, and bring to a boil. Reduce the heat, add all of the clams, and simmer for 6 minutes, covered. Add the cockles to the casserole, stir, cover, and cook for another 4 minutes. Remove from the heat and let cool in the cooking liquid.

Remove the shellfish from the cooking liquid. Allow the liquid to settle, then strain it carefully, leaving any sand deposit on the bottom of the casserole. Set aside.

Open the oysters, delicately remove them from their shells without damaging them, and set them aside in their own water.

LEEK

Cut the leek lengthwise into thin matchsticks (this is called a julienne) and plunge them into a pan of boiling salted water for 3 minutes. Drain, pass quickly under cold running water, and drain again carefully.

FOIE GRAS BUTTER

Cut the foie gras into large cubes and set aside.

Reduce the white wine with the shallots, add a little of the oyster water and some of the reserved cooking liquid from the shellfish. Incorporate the butter bit by bit, whisking as you do so to emulsify the sauce.

Blend this *beurre blanc* with the cubes of foie gras. Check the seasoning and add a dash of sherry to taste.

BEFORE SERVING

Warm the julienne of leek and divide evenly among the plates. Distribute the small whole scallops, the slices of scallop, and the shellfish evenly among the plates and cover the plates with foil. Then place them in an oven preheated to 350°F for a few minutes. Uncover, spoon on the foie gras butter, and serve immediately.

A RECIPE THAT IS BOTH EXTREMELY SIMPLE AND EXTREMELY SOPHISTICATED:
A SYMBOL, FOR ME, OF MY EARLY DAYS AS A COOK. IT'S IMMEDIATE CUISINE, ECONOMICAL
OF ACTION AND MEANS, BUT WITH A STRONG IDEA BEHIND IT: A BEURRE BLANC
THAT IS BOUND USING FOIE GRAS, VERY TASTY AND SMOOTH.

OYSTER JELLY AND DUCK FOIE GRAS
WITH BEET JUICE, RYE BREAD, AND BEAUFORT CHEESE

OYSTER JELLY (FIRST STAGE)

Open the oysters and drain them on paper towels, then lay them in a small plate. Strain off the water and set it aside.

Heat the mussel water. Add the softened gelatin and stir to dissolve. Add the oyster water (about 1¼ cups), and pour the mixture into a glass bowl set in another bowl of ice cubes. Mix gently (without creating bubbles) to cool the preparation. Just when the jelly starts to congeal, coat the oysters with it, by pressing them gently with a fork to drench them in the jelly. Place them one by one on a cold plate. Set aside in the refrigerator.

BEET JUICE

Peel the raw beets and put them through the juicer. Reduce the resulting juice over low heat to about ⅔ cup. Add salt and pepper and allow to infuse for 3 minutes. Strain the juice into a small container and set aside in the refrigerator.

RYE TOAST

Cover the slices of bread with melted butter, then place them under the broiler for 3–4 minutes on each side. Place slices of Beaufort cheese on each slice.

OYSTER JELLY (SECOND STAGE)

Mash the foie gras with a fork. Form six small mounds of the foie gras in each of four soup plates. Gently place a jellied oyster on top of each mound. Cover the plates with plastic wrap and set aside in the refrigerator until ready to serve.

BEFORE SERVING

Take the plates out of the refrigerator and remove the plastic wrap.

Warm the toasts under the broiler for 1 minute.

Spoon some of the reduced beet juice into the center of the four soup plates, and place the toasts on the edge.

Serves 4

OYSTER JELLY

24 OYSTERS

1 SCANT CUP SHELLFISH JUICE (COOKING LIQUID FROM MOULES MARINIÈRES WILL DO)

2 LEAVES OF GELATIN, SOFTENED IN A BOWL OF COLD WATER

7 OUNCES COOKED FOIE GRAS

BEET JUICE

½ POUND RAW BEETS (OR ⅔ CUP BEET JUICE)

SALT AND FRESHLY GROUND PEPPER

RYE BREAD

4 SLICES RYE BREAD

4 TEASPOONS UNSALTED BUTTER, MELTED

4 THIN SLICES BEAUFORT CHEESE

Cliché à l'Anglaise

Thank your lucky stars if ever you get so tired that you have to go to an English country house hotel like Les Quatr' Saisons to recover. Your every need is attended to with a kind of solicitude that one finds almost nowhere else on earth. Butlers hover at every door. The dimensions of the bedrooms are so lordly that you could share one with your aunt Emily and her extended family, without upsetting your peace of mind in the least. Sometime before nightfall you may locate the bed, but only after a methodical search. A day or two later, once you know your way around your vast suite, you may discover that the small gilt decanter on the Chippendale side table is not merely decorative: It contains, to your joy, an old Madeira (Verdelho and Malvasia), which will fortify you henceforth when you return from your walks. The French are generally ignorant of this great wine; they tend to let it gather dust in the cupboard and use it only occasionally to moisten the overcooked veal kidneys they eat with rice as dry as sawdust.

Ten years ago, Raymond Blanc, who runs the Manoir des Quatr' Saisons at Great Milton, Oxfordshire, invited Pierre Gagnaire for three or four days as guest chef. It all worked out wonderfully because, as we are all beginning to understand, Gagnaire's brand of cooking can be exported from France with no difficulty whatsoever. I came along to record the proceedings, doing so in my bedroom in the company of the vintage Madeira, which helped enormously.

But all good things come to an end. Farewell, immaculate lawns of England; farewell, pots of nobly astringent Assam tea; farewell, Madeira; farewell, Raymond Blanc. Shedding a bitter tear, we ordered a taxi for the next morning at dawn. Punctually at six a.m., a cab driver wearing a top hat and cape appeared in the hall of the manor, with the mist swirling mysteriously around him.

Now if there is one aspect of England that I would heartily recommend (apart from vintage Madeira), it is a shrewd selection of the country's most worn-out clichés. Great Milton—a great moment, indeed.

J.-F. A.

MOUSSELINE OF SCALLOPS, ROAST DUBLIN BAY PRAWN (LANGOUSTINE) TAILS,
SQUAB BREASTS IN MUSTARD SAUCE

MOUSSELINE OF SCALLOPS

Purée the scallops in a mixer and push through a *tamis* (a fine-mesh, drum sieve) into a bowl set in crushed ice. Stir in the cream using a spatula. Add the salt, pepper, and vermouth. Pour the mousseline into small buttered timbales and cook in a bain-marie for 20–25 minutes in an oven preheated to 300°F, taking care to protect them with aluminum foil. Wilt the spinach in a little butter for 2–3 minutes. Set aside and keep warm.

LANGOUSTINE TAILS

Split the langoustines, reserving the heads. Remove the flesh, keeping the last two rings on the shell. Cover with plastic wrap and set aside in the refrigerator. Pound the heads roughly and roast them in a casserole with the oil. When they are golden, deglaze with a glass of water, reduce, and pour in the champagne. Reduce by half. Add some chopped parsley leaves and simmer for 10 minutes over low heat. Strain off the juice, which will be thick, strong, and brownish in color. Set aside and keep warm.
Roast the langoustine flesh in a buttered nonstick pan, set aside, and keep warm.

SQUAB BREASTS

Cook the squab carcasses in the chicken stock for 40 minutes, then strain. Brown the seasoned squab fillets with a pat of butter. Take them out while they are still pink and keep them warm on a plate, covered with aluminum foil.
Pour off the cooking fat, deglaze the pan with the squab stock, and reduce by three-quarters. Whisk in the mustard and a pat of butter.
Cut the squab breasts into long, thin slices (*aiguillettes*) and coat them with the reduced mustard *jus*. Set them aside and keep warm.

BEFORE SERVING

Heat up the langoustine *jus*, emulsify with a pat of butter and the heavy cream. Place a small mound of the wilted spinach on each plate, then add the scallop mousseline, a few squab breast slices, and a langoustine tail. Coat the mousseline with langoustine *jus* and serve.

THIS EXTREMELY REFINED SCALLOP MOUSSELINE MARKS A CLEAN BREAK WITH
THE QUENELLES OF DAYS GONE BY, WHICH TO MY TASTE WERE TOO STODGY.
THE SUGARY VANILLA OF THE LANGOUSTINES WITH THE STRONGER-TASTING
SQUAB BREASTS PROVED A DARING COMBINATION; BUT IT REMAINS A SOUND,
WELL-CONSTRUCTED DISH THAT I WOULD HAPPILY REPEAT TODAY.

Serves 4

MOUSSELINE OF SCALLOPS

8 LARGE SEA SCALLOPS (WITHOUT CORAL)

1 SCANT CUP HEAVY CREAM

1 TABLESPOON NOILLY PRAT VERMOUTH

2 TEASPOONS UNSALTED BUTTER

LANGOUSTINE TAILS

4 LARGE DUBLIN BAY PRAWN (LANGOUSTINE) TAILS

1 TABLESPOON OLIVE OIL

1 1/4 CUPS CHAMPAGNE

1 BUNCH FLAT-LEAF PARSLEY LEAVES, CHOPPED

4 TEASPOONS UNSALTED BUTTER

1 TABLESPOON THICK HEAVY CREAM

SQUAB BREASTS

4 SQUABS (ABOUT 4 1/2 POUNDS), BREASTS REMOVED, CARCASSES CRUSHED

1 TABLESPOON OIL

2/3 CUP CHICKEN STOCK (SEE PAGE 190)

1 1/2 TABLESPOONS UNSALTED BUTTER

1 TABLESPOON DIJON MUSTARD

SPINACH

6 CUPS FRESH SPINACH, WASHED, STEMS REMOVED

2 TEASPOONS UNSALTED BUTTER

SALT AND FRESHLY GROUND PEPPER

1985

PAMERICELLI OF SWEETBREADS,
TREVISO SALAD, PRESSED ARTICHOKE CAKE

Serves 4

PAMERICELLI

1 AMPLE VEAL SWEETBREAD

⅔ POUND PUFF PASTRY

2 TABLESPOONS UNSALTED BUTTER

½ TEASPOON CURRY POWDER

½ TEASPOON GROUND TURMERIC

SCANT ½ CUP WHITE PORT

1 GENEROUS CUP HEAVY CREAM

1 EGG, BEATEN WITH A SPOONFUL OF WATER

½ CUP BREAD CRUMBS

ARTICHOKE CAKE

6 ARTICHOKE HEARTS

½ LEMON

1 SCANT CUP RICH VEAL STOCK, MIXED WITH 3 LEAVES GELATIN THAT HAVE BEEN SOFTENED IN COLD WATER

FRYING OIL, PREFERABLY PEANUT OIL

SALT AND FRESHLY GROUND PEPPER

HANDFUL OF TREVISO CHICORY SALAD

½ LEMON

PAMERICELLI

Heat a generous pat of butter in a heavy-bottomed casserole. Add the salted sweetbreads and cook for 15–20 minutes, turning frequently and basting well with the butter. Remove and set aside on a plate.

Discard the cooking butter, add fresh butter and spices, and sauté for 2 minutes. Deglaze with the port and cook until almost entirely evaporated. Add the cream and cook gently for 25 minutes over very low heat. Strain the sauce (it should be full of flavor), and set aside half.

Cut the sweetbreads into large squares, add them to the sauce, and mix gently to coat them well. Remove and cool to room temperature.

Cut the puff pastry into four 6-inch-diameter rounds and place a portion of sweetbreads in the center of each. Wet the edges of the pastries and fold them over to form half-moon packets. Pinch the edges together with thumb and forefinger. Brush the packets with the beaten egg, roll in bread crumbs, and set aside.

ARTICHOKE CAKE

Cook the artichoke hearts with the water, a squeeze of lemon juice, and salt in a pressure cooker for 15 minutes. Drain carefully and slice. Place the slices in layers in a small terrine. Add the well-seasoned veal stock. Cover with foil and cook in a bain-marie for 40 minutes in an oven preheated to 350°F.

Leave the terrine to cool in the refrigerator for several hours. At the last minute, turn out the artichoke cake and slice it thickly—a delicate operation, to be carried out with a very good knife, or even with an electric carving knife.

BEFORE SERVING

Deep-fry the sweetbread packets at 350°F. When they are well browned, drain them on paper towels. Season the treviso leaves with some of the curried sweetbread sauce and a few drops of lemon juice. Arrange them around the edge of the plate, then lay a slice of artichoke cake on top and a hot pamericelli in the center.

THIS NEAT LITTLE RECIPE IS INSPIRED BY EDOUARD NIGNON. THE ARTICHOKE CAKE IS
A REAL FIND. IT'S A SOMEWHAT RICH, DENSE DISH THAT MAKES A SPLENDID ENTRÉE.
TODAY, I THINK I'D ISOLATE THE TWO IDEAS: I'D SERVE THE TERRINE ON ITS OWN,
FOLLOWED BY THE PAMERICELLI WITH A HANDFUL OF FRESH HERBS.

1987

FEUILLETÉ OF TRUFFLES AND PIG'S EARS,
BROAD BEANS AND SALSIFIES (OYSTER PLANT)

Serves 4

PIG'S EARS

4 SQUARES OF BAKED PUFF PASTRY
(FEUILLETÉS), 6 INCHES SQUARE AND 2
INCHES HIGH

2 PIG'S EARS, COOKED IN STOCK

1¼ CUPS RED PORT

1 GENEROUS CUP REDUCED VEAL STOCK

1 CUP THINLY SLICED TRUFFLES

1 TABLESPOON BALSAMIC VINEGAR

CARAMELIZED SALSIFIES

9 OUNCES WASHED AND PEELED SALSIFIES

JUICE OF ½ LEMON

4 TEASPOONS UNSALTED BUTTER

2½ TEASPOONS SUGAR

1 TABLESPOON BALSAMIC VINEGAR

3 TABLESPOONS CHOPPED BLACK TRUFFLE

BROAD BEANS

1 OUNCE SHELLED VERY YOUNG, TENDER,
FRAGRANT BROAD BEANS (THE FIRST OF
THE SEASON)

1½–2 TEASPOONS FLEUR DE SEL

PIG'S EARS

Slice the pig's ears thinly and set aside in the refrigerator. Prepare the sauce: Reduce the port by three-quarters. Bring the veal stock to a boil and add it to the reduced port along with 1¾ ounces of truffle slices. Cook for 3 minutes over low heat, then mix finely to obtain an intensely scented *coulis*. Check the seasoning and sharpen the sauce with a dash of balsamic vinegar.

CARAMELIZED SALSIFIES

Slice the salsifies lengthwise into ½-inch-thick pieces. Cook for 25 minutes in boiling salted water with a squeeze of lemon juice. Drain thoroughly.
Melt a pat of butter in a saucepan, add the salsifies, sprinkle with sugar, and caramelize over gentle heat. Check the seasoning, and add a dash of balsamic vinegar and the chopped truffle. Keep warm in a covered bowl.

BROAD BEANS

Remove the beans from their outer skins and set aside in the refrigerator, covering them with a moist paper towel.

BEFORE SERVING

Cut each of the *feuilletés* into four even squares.
Reheat the slices of pig's ears and coat them with the hot sauce.
Lay a square of puff pastry on each plate, then add some of the caramelized salsifies, truffle slices, and pig's ears with their sauce. Lay another square of pastry on top and repeat the procedure until all the ingredients are used up. Stack the puff pastries as high as possible.
Serve the raw broad beans separately with a little fleur de sel.

THIS IS AN ASTONISHING, IMPROBABLE DISH—PUFF PASTRIES
STACKED TO AN UNBELIEVABLE HEIGHT, TO THE POINT OF TOPPLING OVER—
AGONY TO BRING TO THE TABLE, AND TO EAT! DO THE SALSIFIES FIT IN AS THEY SHOULD?
THEY CERTAINLY OUGHT TO, WITH THEIR DENSE, CHEWY CHARACTER.
AND THEY PROLONG THE IDEA OF THE FEUILLETÉ IN A RATHER DELIGHTFUL WAY.

MENU — NOVEMBER 1988

MOUSSETTE OF YOUNG RABBIT

MARINADE OF CELERIAC AND LEEKS WITH JUNIPER BERRIES

◼

WHOLE ROAST LOBSTER IN ITS SHELL

EMULSIFIED CREAM OF MUSHROOM WITH OLIVE OIL

◼

CARDINE (DAB) AND SWEET PEPPER WITH CARDAMOM

RAW SPINACH JUICE

◼

BOUILLON OF ICED OYSTERS, COMMON CLAMS, AND VENUS CLAMS WITH TAPIOCA

BROCHETTE OF CURRY-FLAVORED SEA SCALLOPS

◼

SQUAB GAUTHIER WITH GREEN FIGS

RED CABBAGE JAM AND ROAST CHOCOLATE PODS

◼

ASSORTMENT OF FARM CHEESES

◼

HOMEMADE DESSERTS AND SWEETMEATS

CARDINE (DAB) AND SWEET PEPPER WITH CARDAMOM,
RAW SPINACH JUICE

SWEET PEPPER

Blacken the bell pepper over an open flame, place it in a plastic bag, and set it aside to steam and cool for 5 minutes. Peel the pepper, rinse with water, and dry with a paper towel. Carefully remove the seeds and cut the flesh into a $1/2$-inch dice. Place the diced pepper in a small heat-proof dish or small saucepan, pour over the stock, and add the butter, oil, crushed cardamom, garlic, and lemon juice. Cook down for 25 minutes over very low heat.

Drain the diced pepper, reserving the liquid.

CARDINE

Place the fish fillets in a small, heavy ovenproof dish and pour over the pepper cooking liquid. Season them with salt and cook in an oven preheated to 350°F for 4–5 minutes. Remove from the oven and let rest for 4–5 minutes at room temperature.

SPINACH JUICE

Purée the spinach leaves with the mineral water. Squeeze the purée through a clean kitchen towel to extract as much juice as possible. Add salt and pepper to the juice, then season with a dash of the pepper cooking liquid.

BEFORE SERVING

Divide the diced pepper among four hot soup plates, add the fish fillets, and pour the spinach juice around.

The *cardine* is a flatfish like a dab with both eyes on the uppermost side of its body. The body is pale brown with brown markings, but only on one side, the other being white. The French also call it *limandelle* by analogy, on account of its lemon hue.

Serves 4

CARDINE AND SWEET PEPPER

4 CARDINE FILLETS OR OTHER WHITE-FLESHED SEA FISH

1 RED BELL PEPPER

1 SCANT CUP WHITE FISH STOCK

2 TEASPOONS UNSALTED BUTTER

3 TABLESPOONS OLIVE OIL

1 CRUSHED GREEN CARDAMOM POD

1 GARLIC CLOVE

JUICE OF $1/2$ LEMON

RAW SPINACH JUICE

7–8 CUPS FRESH SPINACH LEAVES, WASHED, STEMS REMOVED

$1/2$ CUP MINERAL WATER

SALT AND PEPPER

1988

SICHUAN PEPPER–ROASTED SEA SCALLOPS,
TURNIPS BROWNED IN GOOSE FAT, FOIE GRAS AND PEAR DOMINOS SAUTÉED IN BUTTER,
OYSTERS IN BEEF JELLY

Serves 4

PEAR DOMINOS

1 PEAR

4 TEASPOONS UNSALTED BUTTER

PINCH OF SUGAR

3$^1/_2$ TABLESPOONS SHERRY VINEGAR

3$^1/_2$ OUNCES (ABOUT $^3/_4$ CUP) FRESH DUCK
FOIE GRAS, CUT INTO 2-INCH DICE

TURNIPS

7 OUNCES YOUNG TURNIPS

1 TABLESPOON GOOSE FAT

SEA SCALLOPS

8 SEA SCALLOPS, CUT IN HALF
HORIZONTALLY

1 TEASPOON SICHUAN PEPPER, FRESHLY
GROUND

2 TEASPOONS UNSALTED BUTTER, MELTED

FLEUR DE SEL

OYSTERS IN BEEF JELLY

1 SCANT CUP CLARIFIED BEEF CONSOMMÉ

$^1/_2$ LEAF GELATIN, SOFTENED IN
COLD WATER

4 LARGE OYSTERS (SPÉCIALES NO. 1)

$^1/_4$ TO $^1/_3$ CUP RAW ZUCCHINI, CUT IN
$^1/_{16}$-INCH-SQUARE DICE (BRUNOISE)

PEAR DOMINOS

Peel the pear and cut into $^1/_8$-inch dice. Sauté the pieces in a little fresh butter, just until transparent. Add the sugar and vinegar and sauté briefly for 1 minute. Set aside in a small dish.

TURNIPS

Carve the turnips into boat shapes with a paring knife (*tourner*). Blanch the turnips in salted boiling water, drain, and brown slowly in the goose fat for 20 minutes over low heat. Drain the turnips well and set them aside in a container.

SEA SCALLOPS

Rub the scallops with freshly ground Sichuan pepper. Roll them in melted butter, place them in a hot, nonstick frying pan, and cook for 1 minute on each side.

BEFORE SERVING

Arrange portions of foie gras and pears on hot plates. Place the turnips on top and the scallops around them. Sprinkle a little fleur de sel on the scallops.
This dish is delicious accompanied by an oyster in a spoonful of beef jelly (see recipe below).

OYSTERS IN BEEF JELLY

Heat the beef consommé, then add the squeezed, softened leaf of gelatin. Pour into a glass bowl and place in another bowl with ice cubes. Open the oysters, remove them from their shells, and drain carefully.
Lay the oysters in four large spoons, cover them with the beef consommé just as it is beginning to congeal, then sprinkle with the *brunoise* of zucchini.
Place the spoons in a dish and keep them in the refrigerator until you are ready to turn the jelly out on the serving plates alongside the scallops.

OYSTERS IN BEEF JELLY

ZUCCHINI SABLÉS, MOUSSE OF BABY RABBIT WITH JUNIPER BERRIES

GREEN CABBAGE AND LANGOUSTINES WITH SMOKED STURGEON

CREAM OF CAULIFLOWER WITH CUCUMBERS

SLICE OF LOBSTER POACHED IN SPICY BUTTER

ENDIVE STUFFED WITH NUTMEG-SCENTED PUMPKIN

SICHUAN PEPPER—ROASTED SEA SCALLOPS,

TURNIPS BROWNED IN GOOSE FAT, FOIE GRAS AND PEAR DOMINOS SAUTÉED IN BUTTER, OYSTERS IN BEEF JELLY

OVEN-POACHED FILLET OF IRISH SALMON

CHINESE ARTICHOKE MARMALADE WITH SALSIFIES AND MIGNONETTE OF VEAL SWEETBREAD WITH CORIANDER

GRILLED WOOD SQUAB

SPINACH AND WATERCRESS BROTH, CARROTS FLAVORED WITH HONEY AND ALMONDS

FARM CHEESES WITH ALMONDS, RAISINS, NUTS, AND FIGS

HOUSE DESSERTS AND SWEETMEATS

THE TURNIP

THE TURNIP IS THE POOR MAN'S TRUFFLE,

A PRODUCT WRONGLY VIEWED AS DULL, WHICH ON THE CONTRARY

BRIMS WITH CHARACTER IF PROPERLY HANDLED.

GLAZED TURNIPS, TURNIPS WITH SALT OR IN BROTH—ALL ARE GOOD.

THEIR SPECIAL TASTE MAKES THEM A BASIC INGREDIENT OF GOOD COOKING.

Alain Chapel

The modesty of one great chef in the presence of another is something to behold, demonstrating the workings of emotion as well as the emotions of work. Pierre Gagnaire had a deep respect for the late Alain Chapel, so profound in fact that he never dared to go to Chapel's restaurant. The world is such that often we won't cross the thresholds of the people we admire, or even leave our visiting cards on their hall tables.

For chefs of Pierre's generation, Chapel was an enigmatic figure. At Mionnay, where he presided, nearly every dish had an ascetic quality (his *gelée de pigeons ramiers*, for example, or his *huîtres de pleine mer avec leur granité de savagnon*). Alain appreciated Pierre's talent, but there was something about Gagnaire that disturbed the quiet, almost frighteningly solitary classicism of Chapel—a kind of ornamentation, perhaps, an epic profusion that he only half comprehended.

I had spent time with both Chapel and Gagnaire, so I arranged for them to come to my apartment in Lyon and dine together on neutral ground—not for the quality of the cooking, I hasten to say, but for the opportunity to express themselves to each other. Pierre's admiration for Alain was obvious, but Alain blew it off like a puff of smoke from his Montecristo. The modesty of the first was lost in a profusion of compliments, while the other tried uneasily to fend them off.

What can I say? Great creators are as averse to showing their admiration of others as they are to being admired themselves. Eulogies are all too often verbose, whereas silence is seldom, if ever, inelegant. I concluded from this experience that there are certain admirations that should never be disclosed.

In Javier Marias's novel *L'homme sentimental*, a tenor about to go on stage binds his mouth closed with a strip of tape to avoid any threat to his voice before the performance. Likewise, a great chef might handcuff himself before he goes into the kitchen. Cooking is much more than recipes; when you embark upon it you need to be razor sharp, with your energy intact. You have to keep yourself in rigorous training. Pierre Gagnaire goes running early in the morning, every day of his life. Two weeks before the heart attack that killed him, Alain Chapel went on a bicycle trip with his doctor.

The path leading to the greatest cuisine carries its practitioners to phenomenal levels of endeavor. They must rise far above the ordinary human market to which they cater.

J.–F. A.

SUPRÊME OF GUINEA FOWL,
SCENTED WITH CINNAMON AND BRAISED IN GRAPEFRUIT-CUCUMBER MILK AND DARJEELING TEA, COUSCOUS WITH HAZELNUT OIL

GUINEA FOWL

Cut the breasts from the guinea fowl, leaving the skin intact, and remove the thighs (reserve these for another use). Crush and brown the carcass, neck, and feet in a casserole with a little oil. Remove excess fat, add a little water, the thyme, and the bay leaf. Simmer for 35 minutes and cool to room temperature. Strain the resultant broth and refrigerate in a small container.

Slice open the guinea fowl breasts, sprinkle with cinnamon, and close again.

Heat a generous tablespoon of butter in a heavy casserole, add the guinea fowl breasts, skin side down, sprinkle with salt, and brown for 5–6 minutes. Turn them over and cook for 2 minutes more on the opposite side. Remove the breasts from the pan, and discard the cooking fat. Pour in the milk, bring to a simmer, then add the grapefruit peel, the diced cucumber, and the remaining butter.

Poach the guinea fowl breasts in the milk for 20 minutes over low heat. Drain, set the breasts aside in a dish, and keep warm.

Strain the grapefruit peel and cucumbers out of the milk, and pour the milk back into the pan. Add the Darjeeling tea leaves, wrapped in cheesecloth, and allow to infuse for 5 minutes off the heat.

Remove the tea sachet, and reduce the milk by three-quarters over low heat. Season the milk with salt, strain it into a small saucepan, and set aside.

COUSCOUS

Peel the red bell pepper and dice it very small. Soak the raisins in a bowl of hot water and drain them when they are very plump.

Boil 1/2 cup of clear guinea fowl broth and add a touch of salt.

Melt the butter in a saucepan and add the diced pepper, raisins, and couscous. Mix well, then add the hot guinea fowl broth. Cover and leave to expand off the heat. Fluff and separate the couscous with a fork, adding the hazelnut oil drop by drop.

BEFORE SERVING

Reheat the grapefruit milk, blend quickly to bind it, and correct the seasoning. Distribute the couscous among the plates, place half a guinea fowl breast on each, and sauce with the grapefruit-cucumber milk.

GUINEA FOWL IS DIFFICULT TO SELL ON A RESTAURANT MENU. THE IDEA FOR
THIS DISH CAME TO ME WHEN SOMEBODY GAVE ME SOME FABULOUS TEA AS A GIFT.
I TRIED USING IT IN A KIND OF REVERSE INFUSION OF GRAPEFRUIT AND CUCUMBER.
THEN I DISCOVERED THAT TEA AND MILK WORK EXTREMELY WELL WITH GUINEA FOWL.

Serves 4

GUINEA FOWL

1 FARM-RAISED GUINEA FOWL (ABOUT 3 1/2 POUNDS), DRAWN AND DRESSED (RESERVE THE NECK AND FEET)

1 TABLESPOON PEANUT OIL

1 2/3 CUPS WATER

1 SPRIG THYME

1/2 BAY LEAF

2 PINCHES OF GROUND CINNAMON

1 1/2 TABLESPOONS BUTTER

1 2/3 CUPS MILK

ZEST OF 1 ORGANIC GRAPEFRUIT

1/4 CUP CUCUMBER, PEELED AND SEEDED

1 TABLESPOON DARJEELING TEA

COUSCOUS

3/4 CUP COUSCOUS

1 RED BELL PEPPER

2 TABLESPOONS GOLDEN RAISINS

1 TABLESPOON UNSALTED BUTTER

1 TEASPOON HAZELNUT OIL

SALT AND PEPPER

1990

COD "SOCCA" WITH AGED PARMESAN CHEESE,
CRABMEAT, BRUSSELS SPROUT LEAVES, AND SEA SCALLOPS, SEA URCHIN SAUCE
WITH YELLOW JURA WINE

Serves 4

SEA URCHIN AND WINE SAUCE

4 SEA URCHINS

2 TABLESPOONS OLIVE OIL

1¼ CUPS JURA VIN JAUNE

BRUSSELS SPROUTS

½–⅔ POUND BRUSSELS SPROUTS

4 TEASPOONS UNSALTED BUTTER

SALT AND PEPPER

COD "SOCCA"

1 CUP CHICKPEA FLOUR

½ CUP WATER

3½ TABLESPOONS OIL

1¾ OUNCES COD, POACHED AND SHREDDED

2–3 TABLESPOONS GRATED PARMESAN CHEESE

SCALLOPS AND CRAB

4 SEA SCALLOPS

PINCH OF FLEUR DE SEL

FINELY GROUND BLACK PEPPER

5½ OUNCES CRABMEAT (MEAT OF 2 SMALL FRESH CRABS)

2 TEASPOONS UNSALTED BUTTER FOR THE SEA URCHIN CORAL

SEA URCHIN AND WINE SAUCE

Open the sea urchins, remove and set aside the coral. Crush the shells and sauté in a pan with a little oil. Add the wine and 3 glasses of spring water. Simmer for 30 minutes. Allow to rest for a few minutes and strain carefully. Reduce to 1 cup and set aside.

BRUSSELS SPROUTS

Tear off the most substantial leaves from the outside of the sprouts and cook them for 1 minute in a pan of boiling water. Refresh in a bowl of water and ice, drain, and set aside.
Chop the hearts very finely, sweat them off in plenty of butter, and simmer for 20 minutes over very low heat. Incorporate the sea urchin sauce, then continue simmering until you have something close to a purée. Season lightly with salt and add pepper.
At the last moment, warm the outer leaves in a tablespoon of water and a little melted butter.

COD "SOCCA"

Mix the chickpea flour with the water and oil; it should have the texture of crêpe batter.
Ladle some of this mix into a hot, well-oiled frying pan, scatter in a little shredded cod, and cook on high heat for 4 minutes. Place the cooked socca on a small plate and set aside at room temperature. Repeat this process until you have four pancakes (*galettes*) ready.
A few minutes before you bring together the other ingredients, sprinkle the socca pancakes liberally with Parmesan and reheat them in a preheated 325°F oven for 2 minutes.

SCALLOPS

Slice each scallop fairly thickly. At the last moment, sprinkle with fleur de sel and finely ground fresh pepper.

BEFORE SERVING

Spread a spoonful of the Brussels sprout purée over the bottom of each plate. Place a socca pancake on top, spread some warm crabmeat on top of this, and then add the sea urchin coral, which has been heated in a little melted butter. Arrange the outer leaves of the Brussels sprouts decoratively on this construction to give it volume.

RAW MUSHROOM ESSENCE WITH MACE-INFUSED OLIVE OIL,
FLAT GREEN BEANS WITH SEAWEED, SMOTHERED HALF-SMOKED SALMON

Serves 4

HALF-SMOKED SALMON

Coat the salmon steaks with a mix of salt, sugar, and coarsely ground pepper. Cover with plastic wrap and leave to marinate for 1 hour in the refrigerator.

Wipe the steaks of the marinade and lay them on a rack; place the rack in a heavy cast-iron pot containing oak or beech shavings, the allspice, and sprigs of thyme. Place on the fire for about 5 minutes. When the mixture begins to smoke, take it off the fire, cover with a lid, and leave to smoke for 10 minutes.

Remove the rack from the pot. Place the salmon steaks in the refrigerator.

RAW MUSHROOM ESSENCE

Set aside four large, firm mushrooms; chop the remainder with a knife, sprinkle with lemon juice, wrap in a clean kitchen towel, and squeeze out the juice. Set aside in the refrigerator in an airtight container.

Cook the pressed mushrooms in the two oils with the mace for 6–7 minutes. Allow to rest for a few minutes, then strain through a sieve, setting aside the resultant oil. Reserve 2 tablespoons of this scented oil. Add the remainder to the raw mushroom juice and emulsify in the blender.

FLAT GREEN BEANS AND SEAWEED

Cook the crunchy fresh beans in a large pot of boiling salted water. Cool and drain and cut them into small lengths. Cut the kombu seaweed to the same length as the beans.

Form four small bouquets with a mix of seaweed and beans, surrounding each with a strip of blanched leek.

BEFORE SERVING

Cut the mushrooms in thin slices and arrange them on four plates. Place a half-smoked piece of salmon on each plate, then pour mushroom juice over each. Add the bouquet of beans and kombu and season with a little mushroom-flavored oil.

HALF-SMOKED SALMON

4 SALMON STEAKS, SKIN REMOVED, CUT FROM THE HEART OF THE FILLET

1 TABLESPOON COARSE SEA SALT

1 TABLESPOON SUGAR

1 TABLESPOON COARSELY GROUND BLACK PEPPER

OAK OR BEECH SHAVINGS FOR SMOKING THE SALMON

1 TABLESPOON GROUND ALLSPICE

2 SPRIGS THYME

RAW MUSHROOM ESSENCE

$1^{1}/_{8}$–$1^{1}/_{2}$ POUNDS FRESH WHITE MUSHROOMS

JUICE OF 1 LEMON

$1^{2}/_{3}$ CUPS MILD, SWEET OLIVE OIL

SCANT $^{1}/_{2}$ CUP ORDINARY OLIVE OIL

PINCH OF MACE

FLAT GREEN (COCO) BEANS WITH SEAWEED

7 OUNCES LARGE, FLAT, WHITE BEANS

1 OUNCE KOMBU SEAWEED

1 LEEK (GREEN TOP ONLY), BLANCHED

SALT

MACE WAS THE STARTING POINT FOR THIS RECIPE. MACE IS THE OUTER SHELL OR ENVELOPE OF NUTMEG. IT IS VERY STRONGLY SCENTED AND SLIGHTLY BITTER, SO IT NEEDS CAREFUL HANDLING. THE MUSHROOM JUICE WAS A DISCOVERY, INVOLVING A CERTAIN TECHNICAL SLEIGHT OF HAND. THE COMPOSITION AS A WHOLE IS AN ATTEMPT AT SOMETHING SEASONAL THAT DOES NOT RELY ON MEAT JUICES FOR ALL OF ITS FLAVOR. KOMBU, FOR EXAMPLE, IS A HIGHLY SYMBOLIC SEAWEED IN JAPAN. I USE IT OFTEN, RAW AND FINELY CHOPPED.

JOHN DORY GRILLED WITH LEAVES OF LEMON VERBENA,
CUCUMBER IN MELTED HALF-SALTED BUTTER

Serves 4

GRILLED JOHN DORY

4 JOHN DORY FILLETS, SKIN REMOVED

1$^1/_2$ TABLESPOONS HALF-SALTED BUTTER (BEURRE DE BARATTE DEMI-SEL)

2 TABLESPOONS OLIVE OIL

1 BUNCH FRESH LEMON VERBENA LEAVES

CUCUMBER IN MELTED BUTTER

3 TABLESPOONS HALF-SALTED BUTTER

$^3/_4$ OUNCE CURED HAM

ONE 2–2$^1/_2$-INCH-LENGTH EUROPEAN HOTHOUSE CUCUMBER, PEELED (ABOUT $^1/_4$ CUP DICED)

1$^1/_2$ OUNCES FRESH DATES

SALT AND PEPPER

GRILLED JOHN DORY

Place the fish fillets in a small, heavy, ovenproof dish, dab with butter, and sprinkle with olive oil. Add the fresh verbena leaves, cover with plastic wrap, and set aside at room temperature for 30 minutes, turning the fillets over from time to time.

Salt the fillets and cook in an oven preheated to 350°F for 5–6 minutes (depending on their thickness), basting with the hot butter.

Set aside for a few minutes, covered with aluminum foil.

CUCUMBER IN MELTED BUTTER

Dice the ham and the cucumber into small squares. Blanch the cucumber pieces for 2 minutes in boiling salted water. Drain carefully. Cut the dates lengthwise into narrow strips ($^1/_8$–$^1/_4$ inch wide). Set aside all of these ingredients separately in small bowls.

Melt the butter, add the diced ham, diced cucumber, and date strips. Cook for 2 minutes over low heat.

BEFORE SERVING

Place the John Dory fillets in warm soup plates, apportion the mixture of ham, cucumber, and dates on each fillet, and coat generously with the cooking butter, which will be scented with lemon verbena.

TAKE A LOT OF CARE TO COOK YOUR JOHN DORY TO THE
ABSOLUTE MINIMUM—JUST ENOUGH TO GIVE IT THE SLIGHTEST FRIGHT.

The Dual Nature of the Cucumber

Beware of creeping things—soldiers in camouflage, burglars with inhibitions, and dicotyledonous plants—for anything that moves with its belly to the ground is trying to stay out of the limelight, and by definition has something to hide.

In this regard I am not too sure that the cucumber has a clear conscience. For one thing, it sometimes pretends to be a gherkin. It's an easy option—rather too easy, I would say—to sit in a jar while people come at you with wooden pincers as if they meant to shake your hand. And what about the uses of the gherkin: its wary friendship with the terrine, the convivial pot-au-feu, and other such debonair dishes? Beware of all such false camaraderie. In taking on the aspect of a gherkin, the cucumber may be playing a deeper game.

But inspectors Gagnaire and This have made a thorough investigation of the cucumber's true nature. Stripped of its alibis and disguises, we find that it is no more a dicotyledonous plant than Michel Nave, Gagnaire's deputy chef, is a former KGB agent. The cucumber, we can announce here, is in fact a sea creature full of guile. Its unctuous behavior, as it lurks behind the creamy front of who knows what salad, should not deceive us. Nor should its ithyphallic form, which is in the very worst of taste.

Under close interrogation, the cucumber confesses to an origin that anyone with a minimum of imagination might have deduced long ago. For the cucumber exudes the aroma of iodine—the smell of the sea—just as powerfully as Beaufort cheese exudes the scent of Alpine flowers.

Now that we know that the cucumber is an ocean dweller, the chef's work is to plunge it straight back into the salty element without further ado—and preferably in a liquid form that will enhance its iodine propensity. Following his inquiry (which he has since embodied in a recipe), Gagnaire has managed to transform the cucumber into a powerful juice in which delicious little shellfish were made to gambol. Hence his *coques au bain*—a most refreshing, direct, and ingenious dish.

The cucumber has come clean at last.

J.–F. A.

CUCUMBER

IF YOU BOTHER TO QUESTION IT CLOSELY,

THE CUCUMBER ADMITS TO AN ORIGIN THAT NO ONE CAN FAIL TO RECOGNIZE.

YOUR HEALTHY CUCUMBER EXHALES THE SCENT OF IODINE JUST AS POWERFULLY

AS BEAUFORT CHEESE EXUDES THE SCENT OF ALPINE FLOWERS.

MENU — JUNE 1990

CHAUD-FROID OF BABY MACKEREL AND COLD STEWED BABY SQUID
MOUSSELINE OF FRESH PEAS AND CUCUMBERS

■

PAN-FRIED LANGOUSTINES AND PLAICE GARNISHED
WITH SWISS CHARD SCENTED WITH DRIED ORANGE PEEL
SPRING LEEKS WITH HAZELNUT OIL, GREEN CRAB JUICE WITH EPAUTRE

■

LAMB FILLET, TONGUE, AND SWEETBREADS WITH MARJORAM
SHALLOT, EGGPLANT, AND TURNIP CONFIT WITH RATTE POTATOES

■

FARM CHEESE

■

HOUSE DESSERTS AND SWEETMEATS

CHAUD-FROID OF BABY MACKEREL,
COLD STEWED BABY SQUID, MOUSSELINE OF FRESH PEAS AND CUCUMBERS

BABY MACKEREL

Soften the onions in butter over low heat, add the mackerel bones and the thyme, bay leaf, and parsley. Moisten with the wine, vinegar, and 2 glasses of water. Cook for 20 minutes on very low heat, then set aside for a few minutes and strain. Bring the resultant stock to a boil and pour over the mackerel fillets arranged in a dish; add a little oil and cover with plastic wrap. Marinate for 1 hour at room temperature.

Drain the mackerel fillets, then reduce the stock to about $1/2$ cup (it should be quite strong-tasting) and strain it. Mix in the blender with the béchamel and the yogurt, incorporating the rest of the oil drop by drop. Season and set aside in the refrigerator.

At the last moment, gently stir in the whipped cream to create an even smoother texture.

BABY SQUID

Sauté the onion and garlic gently in the oil; incorporate the diced tomato and tomato paste, baby squid, coriander seeds, and herbs. Salt, moisten with a little water and the white wine, and cook for 40 minutes over low heat, adding more water as needed. Allow to cool at room temperature.

At the last moment, correct the seasoning and add a few drops of lemon juice.

MOUSSELINE OF FRESH PEAS

Add the salt to the diced cucumber, and allow the cucumber to drain excess water (*dégorger*) for 30 minutes. Rinse the cucumber pieces under cold running water and pat dry with paper towels.

Cook the peas in a pan of boiling salted water, purée in the blender, and pass through a *tamis* (a fine-mesh, drum sieve). Incorporate the milk and the egg whites, whipped stiff, to obtain a foamy texture. Set aside in the refrigerator.

BEFORE SERVING

Pour a trail of pea mousseline around the rims of the plates. Place a large tablespoonful of thick baby mackerel sauce in the center of each. Serve the stewed squid and the mackerel fillets separately, on smaller plates.

Serves 4

BABY MACKEREL

2 BABY MACKEREL FILLETS (BONES AND HEADS RESERVED)

2 SMALL CHOPPED ONIONS

2 TEASPOONS UNSALTED BUTTER

1 SMALL MIXED BUNCH THYME, BAY LEAF, AND PARSLEY

10 WHOLE BLACK PEPPERCORNS

1 GLASS WHITE WINE (CHARDONNAY)

$3^1/2$ TABLESPOONS WHITE VINEGAR

3 TABLESPOONS OLIVE OIL

1 TABLESPOON BÉCHAMEL SAUCE

$1/2$ POT PLAIN YOGURT

SCANT $1/2$ CUP WHIPPED HEAVY CREAM

BABY SQUID

$10^1/2$ OUNCES BABY SQUID, $1/2$–$3/4$ INCH LONG, CLEANED AND SKINNED

1 SMALL WHITE ONION, CHOPPED

1 GARLIC CLOVE, CRUSHED

2 TABLESPOONS OLIVE OIL

1 TOMATO, PEELED, SEEDED, AND DICED

1 TABLESPOON TOMATO PASTE

10 WHOLE CORIANDER SEEDS

1 BAY LEAF

2 SPRIGS THYME

1 GLASS DRY WHITE WINE (CHARDONNAY)

JUICE OF $1/2$ LEMON

MOUSSELINE OF FRESH PEAS

$3/4$ CUP SHELLED FRESH PEAS

$1/3$ CUP CUCUMBER, PEELED AND CUT INTO SMALL DICE

2 TABLESPOONS COLD MILK

2 WHIPPED EGG WHITES

COLD STEWED BABY SQUID

CUTTLEFISH, SQUID, OCTOPUS—THE CEPHALOPOD FAMILY HAS

ALWAYS DELIGHTED ME WITH ITS GREEDY, ELASTIC CHARM.

THEY MAKE ME THINK OF SUNSHINE AND CHILDHOOD.

EGGPLANT ESSENCE, SHALLOTS, AND VEAL SWEETBREADS
WITH SUMMER TRUFFLES, LACQUERED RABBIT LIVER

Serves 4

EGGPLANT ESSENCE

2 EGGPLANTS

3¹/₂ TABLESPOONS OLIVE OIL

SHALLOTS AND VEAL SWEETBREADS

4 CLUSTERS OF SWEETBREADS (ABOUT 3 OUNCES EACH)

8 SHALLOTS

4 TEASPOONS UNSALTED BUTTER

PINCH OF SUGAR

SALT

2 SUMMER TRUFFLES, FINELY CHOPPED

¹/₂ CUP TRUFFLE JUICE

1 SCANT CUP VEAL ESSENCE

SCANT ¹/₂ CUP WHITE PORT

RABBIT LIVER

2 RABBIT LIVERS

SALT AND PEPPER

2 TEASPOONS UNSALTED BUTTER

PEANUT OIL

2¹/₂ TABLESPOONS BALSAMIC VINEGAR

A FEW LARGE ROMAINE LETTUCE LEAVES

FRESH RASPBERRIES

EGGPLANT ESSENCE

Slice the eggplants lengthwise into ¹/₂-inch-thick slices, using a mandoline. Pan-fry them in a little oil, placing them in a baking dish as you go along. Pour a glass of water into the dish, and bake the eggplant for 30 minutes in an oven preheated to 350°F.

Put the eggplant slices through a juicer, and set aside in the refrigerator in a covered container. The essence should be fruity and slightly bitter to the taste.

SHALLOTS AND VEAL SWEETBREADS

Braise the shallots; then cover them in plenty of butter and add a pinch of sugar. When they are caramelized, add a glass of spring water and cook for 15–20 minutes until they are tender and the juice is syrupy.

Gently brown the sweetbreads in a pan with a pat of butter, and season with salt. Place the sweetbreads in a casserole. Add a little butter, the braised shallots, the fresh truffles, and the truffle juice. Pour in the veal stock, cover, and cook for 20 minutes over low heat, adding the port little by little.

RABBIT LIVER

Season the rabbit livers and brown them lightly in a pan with half of the butter and some oil. Remove the livers, wipe the pan clean with paper towels, then return them to the pan to cook with the remaining butter and the balsamic vinegar. Add some of the cooking juices from the sweetbreads, reduce considerably, and coat the livers with the sauce. Set aside to cool at room temperature.

BEFORE SERVING

Heat the eggplant essence and pour it into four soup plates. Add the sweetbreads on top. Serve, separately, a salad of romaine lettuce with a few crushed fresh raspberries and the rabbit livers, very thinly sliced.

MENU — AUGUST 10, 1991

BOUQUET OF BEANS AND BLACK OLIVES

❧

TURBOT AU CAFÉ
SMALL ONIONS FLAVORED WITH CARDAMOM

❧

OYSTERS SMOTHERED WITH CHANTERELLE MUSHROOMS
CORNET OF ZUCCHINI

❧

EGGPLANT ESSENCE, SHALLOTS, AND VEAL SWEETBREADS WITH SUMMER TRUFFLES
LACQUERED RABBIT LIVER

❧

TOMATO JUICE À L'AURORE
SOFTENED TOMATO

❧

BRAISED SEA BASS WITH LEMON VERBENA, LIME BLOSSOM, SAVIGNY REDUCTION, AND LEMON
EARLY SNAPS

❧

GRILLED PAUILLAC LAMB
BEET AND ZUCCHINI CHUTNEY

The Color of a Croque-Monsieur

French children love the *croque-monsieur*—cheese and ham in a toasted sandwich—and for many youngsters it is the first dish that leads them toward an appreciation of food, and even toward the world of the adult. Cotton candy may have a certain dignity when pressed it into service by sundry great restaurants (Ferran Adriá among them), but it leaves children with less positive memories: indeed, it has come to be considered somewhat tacky due to its association with fairgrounds. But the *croque-monsieur*, and its spinoff the *croque-madame*, nourishes much more substantial appetites and curiosities.

The question of the *croque-monsieur*'s invention can be resolved only by an expert. Dictionaries don't mention it, nor do cookbooks. If a child asks his parents where the *croque-monsieur* got its name, they haven't a clue. They know what it's made of: ham, usually laden with additives; yellowy orange cheese, much of which gets thrown out with the plastic wrapper when the microwave has done its work; and slices of bread, which, when not properly toasted, acquire a suspiciously fleeting tan, like that of a jaundiced man emerging from a session in the tanning salon. But mother and father remain at a loss as to the origin of the word *croque-monsieur*.

Well, here's the answer. The *croque-monsieur* was probably born in a Paris café in the early twentieth century. The monsieur is there purely as a courtesy, the result of a waiter saying, "Voici votre croque, monsieur," or some such. Marcel Proust knew about the item: A character in *Remembrance of Things Past* has one after a concert.

In the following century, *croque-monsieurs* proliferated like mosquitoes in a swamp. Nowadays at certain hours it is—along with the basic sandwich—the only food you can get in a French café. It is the bane of journalists who have to file their stories before 4 or 5 p.m., with work devouring their lunch hour. By the time they get around to eating something, only the bland and rubbery *croque-monsieur* is on offer. When Serge July, the editor of *Libération*, explained that some journalists cannot survive the daily pressure of their lives, he must have been thinking of the resounding thump of *croque-monsieurs* landing on bars on frantic afternoons. News comes at a price.

Imagine our horror, then, when word came down that Pierre Gagnaire was interested in the *croque-monsieur*. This was the stuff of nightmares! Nevertheless, as any brave reporter would, we tried his version of the *croque-monsieur* at Gaya. To begin with, there was no half-tan: the *croque* was coal black. Second, there was no nasty ham, no cheesy drool. Pierre had invented the cuttlefish ink *croque-monsieur*!

We now await the spread of this delicious item to every café worthy of the name. The future of France's daily newspapers depends on it.

J.–F. A.

SAINT-ÉTIENNE
LA RICHELANDIÈRE

1 9 9 2

1 9 9 7

1992

COD WITH A LIGHT BÉARNAISE SAUCE,
SHORE CRAB AND WHEAT SPROUTS, PATTYPAN SQUASH

Serves 4

COD WITH BÉARNAISE

4¹/₂ OUNCES SALT COD FILLET, SOAKED FOR 12 HOURS IN SEVERAL CHANGES OF WATER TO REMOVE EXCESS SALT

1¹/₄ CUPS MILK

4 TEASPOONS UNSALTED BUTTER

5 EGG YOLKS

2 SPRIGS TARRAGON

2 SHALLOTS, FINELY CHOPPED

3¹/₂ TABLESPOONS WHITE VINEGAR

SCANT ¹/₂ CUP WHITE WINE (CHARDONNAY)

1 TEASPOON CRUSHED BLACK PEPPER

1 SCANT CUP CLARIFIED UNSALTED BUTTER (SEE PAGE 191)

CRAB ESSENCE

1¹/₄ POUNDS SHORE (GREEN) CRABS (OR SAND CRABS IF NONE ARE AVAILABLE)

2 TABLESPOONS OLIVE OIL

¹/₃ POUND WHITE FISH (SUCH AS HAKE OR PLAICE)

³/₄ CUP CHOPPED MUSHROOMS

1 GLASS DRY WHITE WINE (CHARDONNAY)

1 LARGE OR 2 MEDIUM TOMATOES, PEELED AND SEEDED

1 TABLESPOON TOMATO PASTE

HANDFUL OF PARSLEY STALKS

1 BRANCH DRIED FENNEL

3 SPRIGS THYME

1 BAY LEAF

1 GARLIC CLOVE

COD WITH BÉARNAISE

Cut the cod fillet into ¹/₂-inch squares. Place them in the boiling milk for 5 minutes. Drain carefully and coat with melted butter.

Separate the egg whites from the yolks. Beat the yolks, and set aside the whites.

Cut the tarragon leaves with scissors as finely as possible.

In a small saucepan, reduce the shallots with the vinegar, white wine, pepper, and half the tarragon over low heat. When no more than a tablespoon of liquid remains, add the beaten egg yolks, whisking the ingredients together over low heat; the result should be a firm, thick foam (the whisk should leave a mark across the bottom of the pan).

Now pour in the melted, clarified butter little by little, continuing to whisk the ingredients. Then strain the béarnaise and keep it warm (86°F maximum) in a bain-marie (double boiler).

CRAB ESSENCE

Crush the crabs and brown with oil in a *cocotte* or casserole. When they begin to take on color, add the chopped fish and the mushrooms, moisten with the white wine, and reduce for 5 minutes. Add the tomatoes, tomato paste, and parsley stems, along with the fennel, thyme, bay leaf, and crushed garlic clove. Pour in enough water to cover, and simmer for 35 minutes.

Put the crab stock through a food mill and strain it into a casserole; reduce by three-quarters, until you have a highly concentrated essence (about 5 tablespoons). Set aside and keep warm.

COD WITH A LIGHT BÉARNAISE SAUCE

PATTYPAN SQUASH

Boil the potatoes for about 15 minutes, and steam the squash. Place the raisins in a bowl of warm water to plump.

Chop the cabbage very finely, place in a bowl, sprinkle with vinegar, and leave for 5 minutes. Drain the cabbage, pressing down hard on it; then drain and add the plumped raisins. Season with a pinch of salt, sugar, and a little oil.

BEFORE SERVING

Whip half of the egg whites with a pinch of salt until stiff.

Mix together the cod and the béarnaise. Very carefully incorporate 8 tablespoons of whipped egg whites and the remaining tarragon.

Peel the potatoes (which should still be hot), cut them into thickish rounds, and divide them among four warm plates. Cut the squashes in half, place 2 halves in each plate, and sprinkle them with olive oil.

As gently as possible, mix together the cabbage salad and the wheat sprouts, and deposit a spoonful over the potatoes. Add a few tablespoons of cod and béarnaise to each plate. Drizzle crab essence around and over them, and serve.

THIS IS AN UNEXPECTED RECIPE, TO SAY THE LEAST. I HAD SOME SALT COD
(A BIT TOO SALTY) AND SOME BÉARNAISE SAUCE (A BIT TOO VINEGARY). OUT OF THESE
TWO MINOR DISASTERS WAS BORN AN AMUSING DISH. FOR ME, BÉARNAISE IS ABOVE ALL
A FINE REDUCTION AND ESSENCE OF TASTES, AND AS SUCH ANYTHING BUT BANAL. IT
MUST BE GIVEN TIME; THE TASTES NEED TO ESTABLISH THEMSELVES WITHIN EACH OTHER—
ALTHOUGH THE IDEA OF MAKING A BÉARNAISE IN ADVANCE SHOULD NEVER BE
CONSIDERED. A REALLY GOOD BÉARNAISE IS MAGNIFICENT. YOU CAN SERVE IT WITH COD,
WITH POLENTA. . . . THE WHIPPED EGG WHITE IS ALSO QUITE UNEXPECTED—
NOW, THAT WAS NEVER DONE IN THE OLD DAYS.

PATTYPAN SQUASH

4 SMALL RATTE (FINGERLING) POTATOES

4 BABY PATTYPAN SQUASH

2 TABLESPOONS GOLDEN RAISINS

6 CUPS WHITE CABBAGE

1 TABLESPOON HOT WHITE VINEGAR

PINCH OF SUGAR

OLIVE OIL

1 GENEROUS CUP WHEAT SPROUTS

SALT AND FRESHLY GROUND PEPPER

AIGRE-DOUX OF SICILIAN TOMATOES,
DUCK BREAST AND SNAILS WITH FRESH BASIL

Serves 4

15 SMALL CHERRY TOMATOES

2 TABLESPOONS OLIVE OIL

1 TABLESPOON MAPLE SYRUP

3¹/₂ TABLESPOONS BALSAMIC VINEGAR

1 DUCK BREAST (MAGRET), CUT IN LARGE PIECES, INCLUDING THE FAT

1¹/₂ TABLESPOONS UNSALTED BUTTER

3 DOZEN PETITS-GRIS SNAILS

SALT AND PEPPER

5 LARGE FRESH BASIL LEAVES, CUT WITH SCISSORS

Pierce each cherry tomato with the tip of a knife. Heat the oil in a pan, add the tomatoes and maple syrup, and cook 8–10 minutes over low heat (they will burst open slightly). Add the balsamic vinegar.

Separately, sauté the duck breasts briefly in the butter, taking care that the meat remains pink. Add the snails, salt to taste, and continue to cook for a few minutes over high heat, to seize the meat.

BEFORE SERVING

Incorporate the mixture of diced duck breast and snails with the tomatoes. Add the basil, mix with care, and put back on high heat for a further 2 minutes. Sprinkle liberally with pepper and serve immediately on well-heated plates.

VEGETABLES AND TASTES OF SUMMER

MINIATURE GRELOT ONIONS GLAZED IN RED CURRANT JUICE
CREMEUX OF CRAB WITH CRISTES-MARINES (SAMPHIRE)

▪

MACAIRE APPLE WITH FRESH ALMOND MILK
LOBSTER BUTTER AND FRESH PEAS

▪

MARMALADE OF CÈPES AND ARTICHOKE WITH CORIANDER, CINNAMON, AND LEMON BALM
TEMPURA OF FRESH ZUCCHINI AND CELERY LEAVES

▪

MARINIÈRE OF RED PEPPERS WITH LIGHTLY SALTED ANCHOVIES
PAN-FRIED SQUID WITH DRIED GARLIC

▪

AIGRE-DOUX OF SICILIAN TOMATOES
DUCK BREASTS AND SNAILS WITH FRESH BASIL

▪

GRILLED SWEETBREADS EN COCOTTE WITH SAGE AND LEMON THYME
PERLÉ VEAL JUICE AND VEAL KIDNEY

▪

ARAVIS SUCKLING KID WITH DRIED ORANGE
SARASSON OF YOUNG LEEK GREENS

▪

ICED PARFAIT FLAVORED WITH LAVENDER
COMPOTE OF WHITE PEACHES WITH NATURAL CANE SUGAR, DOUBLE VANILLA ZABAGLIONE

TOMATO AIGRE-DOUX

BETWEEN SWEET AND SALTY, THE TIPPING POINT IS FRAGILE AND TENUOUS,

YET VERY REAL. THE TRUE ART OF THE COOK RESTS ON THIS SUBTLE BALANCE.

"LAMPARO" BLUE FISH,
MACKEREL, SEARED SARDINES AND ANCHOVIES, OCTOPUS SOUP WITH GREEN PEPPERS

Serves 4

"LAMPARO" BLUE FISH

4 SARDINES

2 TEASPOONS SUGAR

1/2 GLASS PLUS 1 TABLESPOON SHERRY VINEGAR

SCANT 1/2 CUP SOY SAUCE

2 MACKEREL

3 GLASSES WHITE WINE (CHARDONNAY)

SCANT 1/2 CUP WHITE WINE VINEGAR

2 SPRIGS THYME

1 BAY LEAF

5 WHOLE BLACK PEPPERCORNS

2 CAYENNE PEPPERS

SALT

8 FRESH ANCHOVIES

SCANT 1/2 CUP OLIVE OIL

1 GARLIC CLOVE, CRUSHED

PINCH OF ESPELETTE PEPPER

OCTOPUS SOUP

1 OCTOPUS (FROZEN BEFOREHAND TO TENDERIZE IT)

3 1/2 TABLESPOONS VINEGAR

1 LARGE GREEN PEPPER

1 ONION

2 GARLIC CLOVES, CRUSHED

1 LEMON

3 TABLESPOONS OLIVE OIL

3 TOMATOES, PEELED AND SEEDED

1 BOUQUET GARNI (PARSLEY, THYME, AND BAY LEAF, TIED WITH A LEEK)

"LAMPARO" BLUE FISH

Fillet the fish, carefully removing all small bones with tweezers.

Caramelize the sugar, deglaze with the tablespoon of sherry vinegar and the soy sauce, and reduce for 2 minutes. Brown the sardines in a nonstick skillet, skin side down. Turn them into a small ovenproof dish and lacquer with the caramelized sauce. Bake for 25 minutes in an oven preheated to 200°F, basting regularly.

Boil the white wine and white wine vinegar with the thyme, bay leaf, peppercorns, cayenne pepper, and salt. Remove from the heat and soak the mackerel fillets in this preparation for 5 minutes. Drain and set aside on a plate, covered with plastic wrap.

Immerse the anchovies briefly in a bowl of warm water with the half-glass of sherry vinegar added. Rinse them well, then lay them in a heat-proof serving plate. Heat the oil with the well-crushed garlic and a pinch of Espelette pepper, then pour it, burning hot, over the anchovy fillets. Allow to cool at room temperature.

OCTOPUS SOUP

Drop the octopus into a saucepan of boiling salted water with the vinegar added, and simmer for 25 minutes. Drain, remove the beak and the black parts, then dice fairly small.

Sear the pepper over an open flame and place in a plastic bag to steam and cool. When cool, remove the skin and dice. Chop the onion and the garlic. Peel the lemon and carefully remove the segments; set them aside. Cook the onion, diced pepper, and garlic in the oil until soft. Add the octopus pieces and stew for 4–5 minutes. Add the tomatoes, the bouquet garni, and the lemon segments. Moisten with 2 glasses of water and continue to cook for 2 more hours over very low heat. The result should be very thick and concentrated, almost like marmalade. Let cool at room temperature.

BEFORE SERVING

Emulsify a glass of mackerel stock with the anchovy oil and pour into 4 teacups. Arrange the fish on warmed dinner plates. Serve the cold soup separately, in bowls.

IT TOOK ME YEARS TO BRING THIS IDEA TO FRUITION. I COULD NEVER QUITE FIND THE RIGHT TONALITY TO EXPRESS ALL THE RICHNESS OF THESE FISH WHEN THEY ARE IN SEASON. THE IDEA OF 'BLUE FISH' INTERESTED ME: BLUE EQUALS SUMMER FOR ME. AND I LIKED THE 'LAMPARO' IDEA. I DREAMED OF A DISH CONSTRUCTED OF BLUE THINGS—IT COULD INCLUDE TUNA, SCAD, EVEN SEA BASS . . . ALWAYS WITH THE OCTOPUS SOUP AS A VERY DENSE, VERY POWERFUL FOIL.

Frogs and Their Uses

In general, I think, frogs are less suited to the recipes of great culinary art than they are to proverbs. The French say "every frog finds his toad," which may not be politically correct, but is at least explicit. Cooks, who are pragmatists by and large, prefer to say that "every pot has its lid"—which, aside from one or two minor allusions in the toad proverb, amounts to the same thing.

The frog's culinary future looks bleak. Traditionally frogs are pulled out of ponds, chopped in two, divested of their breeches, sautéed in butter, and served piping hot, with a pungent *persillade*. They may also be smothered in garlic so that their memory lingers long after you have risen from the table. When this happens, even the best *chartreuses* and *tarragones*, famed for their digestive qualities, can do little for you. Beware of frogs then, the "reines des étangs" (pond queens) of La Fontaine, because before you know it they will have you in their thrall.

And that's just the fresh version. There are also the frozen frogs—the ones with a pebbly finish, Rubensian thighs, and detergent-like taste, the ones that enemy nations routinely export to us. And after these come the bullfrogs of America, whose massive parts can be grilled like fillet steaks.

Many a chef has attempted a resurrection of the frog as an acceptable food. Patrick Guenon—who deserves to be better known—hit on something very good when he dropped frogs into a Berthoud fondue tempered with cumin, *oeufs persillés*, and St. George's mushrooms. That was really something.

In his still classical, though no longer academic, early years at Saint-Priest-en-Jarez, Pierre Gagnaire came up with a delectable *tourte de grenouilles aux morilles* on the same day that he offered us a *sauté d'agneau à l'anchoiade*. It came with a *sauce rouennaise*, or something of the sort, and it was a princely dish. It is likely that today's frog sanctuaries would no longer allow such a marvel, and in any case the great man in the rue Balzac would probably find its preparation too trivial. Nevertheless, I would like to propose the frog as an example of something that everyone ought to know, but that most people pretend not to know: namely, that Pierre is also a great classical chef.

Only a fool would dare deny it.

J.–F. A.

On Cell Phones

Once upon a time, even the harshest critics of a world gone mad with technology still viewed the telephone as something convivial. Even Ivan Illich, the great critic of modern culture, had plenty to say in its favor. One can only imagine, however, what he would make of the cell phone, a modern scourge that constantly reinvents itself, selling new, repackaged forms of itself on an ongoing basis. The cell phone is the one calamity in our history that has smitten practically every level of the population in equal measure, from adolescents right through to those unfortunate elderly who may be far gone in other ways but can still hear. All, needless to say, are now under strict surveillance. Every more or less functioning ear in the nation is in the same boat, with the exception of the newborn (who have noisy rattles instead).

Pierre Gagnaire uses a cell phone that allows him to communicate instantly from the right bank of the Seine to the left, from Paris to London, from Tokyo to Hong Kong, and so on. I will not reveal his number; half the Western world and a good part of Asia knows it already. The telephone rings in his ears like some mad fire alarm, as if he were the victim of a gigantic clockmakers' conspiracy. So conversation with him is now a problem. In the last few months, the only time we have engaged in continuous conversation was in the Channel Tunnel, where callers can't get at him. For once, we weren't interrupted.

Naturally the incoming calls reach a crescendo during rush hour, between 6:30 and 8:00 p.m., when the faintest lull is like the flight of several thousand ortolans down the rue Balzac. This situation will no doubt continue for many years, until a time when no one will remember those wonderful decompression chambers that we used to call phone booths.

J.–F. A.

ROAST ST. MALO BAY ABALONES,
PETIT PÊCHE OF MUSSELS, COCKLES, DOG-COCKLES,
MACKEREL, AND COD WITH CRACKLING LARD, SAUCE DIABLE

COD WITH LARD

Soak the cod fillet for 12 hours, a day in advance, to extract the salt. Dry well, wrap in plastic wrap, and place in the freezer.

On the day you plan to serve the dish, shave the frozen cod, using a potato peeler, into thin twists and return to the freezer in a dish covered with plastic wrap.

Lay the cooked lard cut into thin slices ($1/16$–$1/8$ inch) on a baking sheet covered with parchment paper. Dry for 2 hours in an oven preheated to 275°F.

ROAST ABALONES

Remove the abalones from their shells and hammer them flat to tenderize them. Rub a frying pan with the lard and heat well. Sear the abalones for 2 minutes on each side. Dab their top sides with butter, sprinkle with grated lemon peel, and leave in an open oven for 20–30 minutes in a container covered with aluminum foil, to keep them warm.

PETIT PÊCHE

Brown the shallot in the butter. Add the mussels, cockles, dog cockles, and white wine. Cover and cook for 5–6 minutes on low heat. Set aside for a few minutes to cool, then remove the shells and strain the juice very carefully to remove any sand.

Dice the mackerel fillets, mix them in with the warm shellfish, and put them into a storage container. Moisten with a glassful of shellfish juice and reserve.

SAUCE DIABLE

Reduce the vinegar and white wine with the chopped shallots, pepper, and tarragon. When there is no more than a tablespoon of liquid left, moisten with the veal essence, tomato marmalade, and shellfish stock. Cook for 15 minutes more. Strain, season with salt and cayenne pepper, and mix in a pat of butter.

BEFORE SERVING

Slice the abalones into thin strips. Reheat the *petit pêche* for 1–2 minutes in the shellfish stock in an oven preheated to 350°F, and pour into hot soup plates. Arrange the strips of abalone and the twists of crunchy lard as attractively as possible. Serve the sauce in a separate dish.

Serves 4

COD WITH LARD

$2^1/2$ POUNDS THICK COD FILLET

$1^3/4$ OUNCES LARD STRIPS, COOKED GENTLY IN WATER UNTIL SOFT

ROAST ABALONES

4 ABALONES

LARD FOR THE FRYING PAN

4 TEASPOONS UNSALTED BUTTER

ZEST OF $1/2$ LEMON

PETIT PÊCHE

2 TEASPOONS UNSALTED BUTTER

7 OUNCES MUSSELS

7 OUNCES COCKLES

7 OUNCES DOG-COCKLES (AMANDES)

1 SMALL MACKEREL, FILLETED

1 SHALLOT, CHOPPED

1 GLASS WHITE WINE (CHARDONNAY)

SAUCE DIABLE

$1/2$ GLASS WINE VINEGAR

1 GLASS WHITE WINE (CHARDONNAY)

1 SHALLOT, CHOPPED

1 TEASPOON CRUSHED BLACK PEPPER

2 SPRIGS TARRAGON

$1^2/3$ CUPS VEAL EXTRACT (DEMI-GLACE)

$1/2$ TEASPOON TOMATO MARMALADE

SALT

PINCH OF CAYENNE PEPPER

1 TABLESPOON UNSALTED BUTTER

LARD COLONNATA

"

I HAVE A PRECISE MEMORY OF MY FIRST TASTE OF COLONNATA LARD:

IT WAS SHAVED ON SLICES OF BREAD. IT WAS AT LE CIRQUE IN NEW YORK,

AND I'VE NEVER FORGOTTEN IT. COLONNATA LARD IS AT ONCE LEAN AND FAT, STRONG AND MILD,

WITH AN UNCTUOUS, LINGERING AFTERTASTE—A TRUE DELIGHT.

MARINIÈRE OF BELON OYSTERS

PALOURDES (CARPET SHELLS) AND SEA SCALLOPS, FROTHY CREAM OF CABBAGE SOUP

BRETON LOBSTER À LA VANILLE

BOUQUET OF BULBOUS CHERVIL

SAUTÉED BABY SQUID AND VENETIAN TAGLIARDIS

CREAM OF SEA URCHIN WITH AGED MALT WHISKY

ÉTUVÉE OF ASPARAGUS

ENOKIS AND JUDAS EAR MUSHROOMS, PUMPKIN MOUSSELINE

GRILLED "COFFEE AND CARDAMOM" VEAL SWEETBREADS

COUSCOUS WITH PEPPER-FLAVORED OLIVE OIL

WHOLE ROAST BRESSE CAPON

TURNIP CAKE, CHESTNUT JUICE SCENTED WITH VINTAGE MARC DE BOURGOGNE

FARM CHEESES

HOUSE DESSERTS

GRILLED "COFFEE AND CARDAMOM" VEAL SWEETBREADS,
COUSCOUS WITH PEPPER-FLAVORED OLIVE OIL

VEAL SWEETBREADS

Heat the oil and clarified butter in a heavy-bottomed casserole. Add the sweetbreads and brown for 15 minutes, turning regularly and basting with the cooking fats. The sweetbreads are done when they are crusty, almost grilled-looking on the outside, but still soft inside. Set aside on a dish and keep warm.

Discard the cooking fat, then pour the coffee into the casserole and add the butter and crushed cardamom. Reduce the liquid by three-quarters. Return the sweetbreads to the pot and coat them with the coffee-flavored butter. Add a little salt and pepper, set aside again, and keep warm.

COUSCOUS

Heat 1/2 cup water with the oil and a pinch of salt. When the water boils, pour in the couscous, cover, and leave to expand off the heat.

Stir the couscous with a fork to separate the grains, adding small quantities of butter bit by bit. Once this is done, incorporate the olives and chopped parsley.

BEFORE SERVING

Mound a generous helping of couscous onto each plate to make a base, then place half a sweetbread onto each and coat generously with the reduced coffee-butter.

Serves 4

VEAL SWEETBREADS

2 SWEETBREAD CLUSTERS, WELL BLANCHED

1 TABLESPOON PEANUT OIL

2 TEASPOONS CLARIFIED
UNSALTED BUTTER

2 CUPS ESPRESSO COFFEE

2 TEASPOONS UNSALTED BUTTER

1 CRUSHED CARDAMOM POD

SALT AND PEPPER

COUSCOUS

1/2 CUP COUSCOUS

DASH OLIVE OIL

2 TEASPOONS UNSALTED BUTTER

1/4 CUP PITTED GREEN OLIVES, SLIVERED

2 SPRIGS FLAT-LEAF PARSLEY, LEAVES
COARSELY CHOPPED

1994

CARPACCIO OF CUMIN-ROASTED PEKIN DUCK,
SANGUETTE WITH STEWED SHALLOTS AND YOUNG LEEKS

Serves 4

PEKIN DUCK

1 SMALL, LEAN-BREASTED DUCK

1 TEASPOON GROUND CUMIN

1 TEASPOON PAPRIKA

3¹/₂ TABLESPOONS OLIVE OIL

1 WHITE ONION, FINELY CHOPPED

4¹/₂ CUPS CHICKEN STOCK

1 BOUQUET GARNI (PARSLEY, THYME, AND
BAY LEAF, TIED WITH A LEEK)

4 TEASPOONS CLARIFIED
UNSALTED BUTTER

LEEK

1 YOUNG LEEK

2 TEASPOONS UNSALTED BUTTER

STEWED SHALLOTS

2 SMALL SHALLOTS

2 TEASPOONS UNSALTED BUTTER

SALT

1 BAY LEAF

BLOOD SAUSAGE SAUCE

COOKING JUICES FROM THE DUCK

1 TEASPOON CORNSTARCH

1³/₄ OUNCES BLOOD SAUSAGE

SALT AND FRESHLY GROUND PEPPER

PEKIN DUCK

The day before:

Remove the duck's thighs, leaving the breast intact. Rub the breast well with the cumin and paprika, baste with oil, cover with plastic wrap, and leave to marinate for 24 hours.

Crush the remaining bones and the thighs and brown in a large casserole with a dash of oil. Discard the cooking fat, add the onion, and brown for 5 minutes. Moisten with the chicken stock, add the bouquet of thyme, bay leaf, parsley, and leek, and cook for 45 minutes. Let rest for 15 minutes, then strain the stock and reduce to about 1 cup. Set the stock aside in the refrigerator for the night.

The next day:

Sear the duck breast in a frying pan with a little oil and clarified butter (make sure the duck stays very pink, almost raw inside). Set aside in a warm place such as an oven with the door ajar, standing in a plate covered with foil. This resting period is important if the meat is to remain perfectly colored.

LEEK

Chop the leek into four 1¹/₄-inch-long pieces. Cook for 6–7 minutes in a saucepan of boiling salted water. When white, drain carefully and place in a small, ovenproof dish with a pat of butter. At the last minute, reheat in an oven preheated to 350°F for 5 minutes.

STEWED SHALLOTS

Place the shallots in a small heavy-bottomed pot with a little butter and cook slowly until golden. Cover with chicken stock and add a little more butter, a pinch of salt, and a bay leaf. Cook for 35 minutes on low heat; the shallots should be very soft, almost melting.

BLOOD SAUSAGE SAUCE

Bring the duck stock to a boil and thicken with the cornstarch. Incorporate the blood from the *boudin* and put the mixture through the blender. Add the shallots, check the seasoning, and set aside to keep warm in a bain-marie.

BEFORE SERVING

Remove the duck breasts from the carcass. Slice them into long, thin lengths (*aiguillettes*)—they should be very pink—then put the lengths together in small bunches. Pour the smooth blood sauce onto four heated plates, add the cooked leek, and pile the *aiguillettes* on top. Sprinkle with pepper, and serve immediately.

MENU — MARCH 1994

CARPACCIO OF CUMIN-ROASTED PEKIN DUCK

SANGUETTE WITH STEWED SHALLOTS AND YOUNG LEEKS

■

LAKE LÉMAN CHAR POACHED IN AN INFUSION OF LEMON THYME AND APPLE JUICE

FRESH MORELS

■

SAUTÉ OF SMOOTH VENUS CLAMS (VERNIS), BABY SQUID, AND RED GURNARD (GALINETTE) WITH SUMAC

RED MULLET SOUP WITH ARTICHOKES

■

CREAM OF PEA SOUP WITH GREEN TEA

BREBIS VELOUTÉ TART, CLEAR BEEF JELLY SCENTED WITH LEMON BALM

■

GRILLED LANGOUSTINE WITH RABBIT'S LIVER AND KIDNEYS

FRESH CORIANDER MACERATED WITH DRIED ORANGE, LETTUCE STUFFED WITH PISTACHIO AND TOMATO PASTE

■

SWEETBREADS, NOISETTE, BREAST AND CUTLET OF PAUILLAC LAMB, ROASTED WITH FRESH HAY

BUCKWHEAT GALETTE WITH BONE MARROW, RED PEPPERS, AND WHITE KIDNEY BEANS

■

FARM CHEESES

■

PIERRE GAGNAIRE'S DESSERTS

1994

CONFIT OF MILK-FED VEAL BREAST SCENTED WITH LEMON BALM AND LEMONGRASS,
TERRINE OF BABY SQUID STUFFED WITH MAPLE SYRUP CHUTNEY

Serves 6

MILK-FED VEAL BREAST

1 MILK-FED VEAL BREAST, ON THE BONE

1 GLASS WHITE WINE

SCANT ¹/₂ CUP OLIVE OIL

1 BOUQUET LEMON BALM,
LEAVES CHOPPED

FRESHLY GROUND PEPPER

4 TEASPOONS UNSALTED BUTTER

1 CARROT, COARSELY CHOPPED

1 ONION, COARSELY CHOPPED

1 CELERY STALK, COARSELY CHOPPED

3 GARLIC CLOVES

3 STALKS LEMONGRASS

2¹/₈ CUPS CORSICAN MUSCATEL WINE

1 SCANT CUP VEAL ESSENCE

1 BAY LEAF

2 SPRIGS THYME

PINCH OF COARSE SEA SALT

JUICE OF ¹/₂ LEMON

1 SMALL BUNCH CHIVES

VEAL BREAST

The evening before:

At least 12 hours in advance, place the veal breast in a deep dish. Add the white wine, oil, half of the chopped lemon balm, and freshly ground pepper. Cover with plastic wrap and leave to marinate in the refrigerator overnight, turning over once or twice.

The next day:

Heat a dash of oil and some butter in a large, heavy casserole, and color the meat on both sides. When the meat is golden, remove it, discard the cooking fat, and add a fresh pat of butter to the pan, along with the carrot, onion, celery, garlic, the remaining chopped lemon balm, and the stalks of lemongrass. Soften for 5 minutes over low heat.

Place the meat on top of the vegetables. Cover and simmer on low heat, moistening with the muscatel little by little as the cooking progresses. When the sauce is completely reduced, pour in 2 glasses of water, and add the veal essence, bay leaf, thyme, and sea salt. Cover again, and cook for 2 hours in an oven preheated to 350°F. Allow to cool. Remove the meat from the bones and slice it into 18 pieces ³/₄-inch thick (3 per person).

Strain and degrease the cooking juices and reduce by three-quarters. Check the seasoning, sharpen with a few drops of lemon juice, and leave the sauce to cool at room temperature.

Brush the slices of meat with the reduced sauce and stack them in threes. Trim their sides to obtain 6 neat rectangles. Truss them together with blanched chives, cover with plastic wrap, and set aside at room temperature.

CONFIT OF MILK-FED VEAL BREAST

BABY SQUID WITH CHUTNEY

Dice the zucchini, tomatoes, pineapple, and onions fairly small. Soften them in a pan with a little butter. Pour over the maple syrup and vinegar, then add the star anise and the preserved lemon, sliced in thin strips. Cook on very low heat for 1 hour, then transfer the chutney into a small dish. Stuff the squid with this mixture and close and secure them with a toothpick. Place them in a terrine with a little butter and the cooking juices from the veal. Place the terrine in a bain-marie and cook for 1 hour in an oven preheated to 325°F. Leave to cool. It is advisable to make the chutney in advance and keep it in the refrigerator for 2 or 3 days.

BEFORE SERVING

The slices of veal breast and the squid should be served at room temperature. Place the veal slices, coated with the sauce, on six plates and serve the squid separately in their terrine.

PRESERVED LEMON

Blanch the organic lemons (no pesticides in the skins!) in a saucepan of boiling water. Repeat this process three more times. Then cut the lemons in quarters, put them back in the saucepan with the mineral water, sugar, and salt. Leave them to stew for $1\frac{1}{2}$ hours over very low heat.

BABY SQUID WITH CHUTNEY

12 SMALL SQUID, CLEANED AND GUTTED

1 ZUCCHINI

1 TOMATO, PEELED AND SEEDED

2 SLICES FRESH PINEAPPLE

4 SMALL WHITE ONIONS

4 TEASPOONS UNSALTED BUTTER

5 TABLESPOONS MAPLE SYRUP

2 TABLESPOONS SHERRY VINEGAR

1 PETAL STAR ANISE

SCANT $\frac{1}{2}$ CUP VEAL COOKING JUICES

PRESERVED LEMON

2 ORGANIC LEMONS

$1\frac{1}{4}$ CUPS MINERAL WATER

$\frac{1}{4}$ CUP SUGAR

1 TEASPOON SALT

FRESHLY GROUND PEPPER

CONFIT OF MILK-FED VEAL BREAST SCENTED WITH LEMON BALM AND LEMONGRASS

THIS DISH IS REALLY A VARIATION ON A VEAL TERRINE, AND AS SUCH IT MAKES AN IDEAL COLD MAIN DISH.

EVERYTHING HINGES ON SOFTNESS AND SMOOTHNESS—THE PERFECTLY BRAISED MILK-FED VEAL, THE SQUID . . . .

Faux Débats

Roland Barthes once wrote that the duty of the intellectual was "to distance society from its time." Well, the duty of a great chef is to be in advance, if only a very little, of the evolution of our awareness of food. In this capacity, he would resolutely turn away from all the clichés of restaurant cuisine, whether *foie gras poêlé*, risotto taken out of its family context and served tepid, or the wretched marriage of tomato and mozzarella.

By the same token, we must stand firm against those who pretend to be in the vanguard of today's cuisine simply because a few nonentities have described them as up and coming. These are the clowns who strike the chords that make the East and West vibrate, who surround their line-caught mackerel with wasabi and the like, who treat the emulsifying process as if it were a new feature of the decathlon, thereby creating some new kind of conceptual art. "We must live in our own time," they tell you. "Nobody drives a Deux Chevaux anymore."

Well. In the deafening pandemonium of today's international cuisine, we would like to know exactly what signs there are of genuine modernity. At this point, the only novelty seems to be that our language and culture are becoming impoverished at breakneck speed.

We would compare cooking not to a car but to an articulated language, a language with its own vocabulary, punctuation, and syntax that lend coherence to all its phrases—or, rather, to all the phases of a good meal. It encompasses those vital old terms that deserve to be saved from obsolescence, as well as those neologisms that, after close examination of what we already have, might just prove to be essential. In this sense, a cook might have recourse to scholarly language as well as to slang, to an English term as well as to a Franco-Provençal one. The most appropriate word could just as easily be drawn from a local dialect as from Latin.

Another *faux débat* that threatens the pleasure of great cuisine consists in the idea that you eat much better in one establishment than in another, when the last time you went to the one you favor was last week and the last time you went to the one you condemn was a decade back. Comparison, as Freud said, is a form of neurosis, but it continues unabated in the modern world. One thing is clear: A good meal is sufficient unto itself. After all, if I wanted to see a revival of a film directed by John Ford, the fact that it was double billed with a film by Claude Lelouch wouldn't influence my decision to go to the cinema.

Yes, I know the two are not in the same category. All the more reason.

J.–F. A.

FARMHOUSE JELLY WITH MACVIN,
FOIE GRAS WITH PEPPERCORNS AND FIG PASTE, LEEK SEQUENCE WITH CORNES DE CERF

Serves 6

FARMHOUSE JELLY

2 CARROTS

1 ONION

14 OUNCES CALF'S TAIL (OR SUBSTITUTE OXTAIL)

RAW HAM KNUCKLE OR TRIMMINGS (ASK YOUR BUTCHER)

1/2 POUND BREAST OF VEAL

1 BOUQUET GARNI (PARSLEY, THYME, AND BAY LEAF, TIED WITH A LEEK)

1 BUNCH FRESH WHITE GRAPES

1/2 BOTTLE MACVIN DU JURA

2 LEAVES GELATIN, SOFTENED IN COLD WATER

FOIE GRAS

1 1/2 POUNDS RAW DUCK FOIE GRAS

10 WHOLE BLACK PEPPERCORNS

1 GLASS AMONTILLADO SHERRY

2 1/4 POUNDS GOOSE FAT

FIG PASTE

1 1/4 CUPS DRIED FIGS

1 1/2 TEASPOONS MACVIN

1/2 VANILLA BEAN, SPLIT IN TWO AND SCRAPED

BLACK SARAWAK PEPPER, GROUND IN A PEPPER MILL

FARMHOUSE JELLY

Prepare a vegetable stock: Dice the carrots and the onion fairly coarsely, and place them in a casserole with the calf's tail, the ham knuckle, and the bouquet garni. Moisten with 1 quart of water and bring to a boil, skimming assiduously. Add the grapes and leave to simmer for 2 hours over very low heat. Allow to settle for a while, then strain the stock without disturbing it too much and put in the refrigerator to cool for 2 hours.

Degrease the stock, carefully removing the fatty layer on its surface, and reduce it by half. Add the macvin and softened gelatin and mix well. Pour the resultant stock into a container and set aside in the refrigerator.

FOIE GRAS (PREPARE 4 OR 5 DAYS IN ADVANCE)

Devein the foie gras and stud it with peppercorns. Place it in a deep dish, sprinkle with salt, then pour the glass of sherry over it. Cover with plastic wrap and leave to marinate for 2 hours in the refrigerator.

Immerse the foie gras in the melted goose fat, raise the temperature gradually to 125°F, and cook for 40 minutes. Allow to settle for a while, then place the foie in a small porcelain terrine. Cover with the cooking fat and place in the refrigerator for 4 or 5 days.

FIG PASTE

The day before:
Put the dried figs in a bowl with the macvin and amontillado sherry to macerate overnight.

The next day:
Blend the macerated figs with a little of the fat used in cooking the foie gras, the vanilla, and 3 tablespoons of melted farmhouse jelly. Pepper freely.

FARMHOUSE JELLY WITH MACVIN

LEEK SEQUENCE

Cut off the green parts of the leek, slice them very fine, and plunge them in boiling salted water for a few minutes. Drain, then soften them in 2 tablespoons of the fat used to cook the foie gras. Add the diced dried tomatoes, capers, and onions, mixing the ingredients together thoroughly. Cook for about 20 minutes over low heat; the final texture should be similar to chutney. Set aside in the refrigerator in a covered container.

Open up 2 leeks (the white part, about 6 inches long), separate the leaves, and plunge them in a large saucepan of boiling salted water. Drain and pat dry with paper towels. Baste the leeks with melted butter and spread them out on a silicone mat. Dry for 3 hours in an oven preheated to 150°F.

Cut 6 thick slices of the white part of the remaining leeks, cook them for 12 minutes in boiling salted water, and drain.

BEFORE SERVING

Cut the foie gras into thick, generous pieces. Season the salad leaves with a little warm goose fat and a dash of lemon juice.

Lay a piece of foie gras, a little jelly, a roll of warm fig paste, and a serving of the leeks in their various forms on each of six large, warmed plates. Arrange the seasoned salad leaves as you see fit. Just before serving, sprinkle the foie gras with a little fleur de sel and freshly ground pepper.

LEEK SEQUENCE

4 LEEKS (STRAIGHT AND NOT TOO THICK)

$1/3$ CUP DRIED TOMATOES

1 TABLESPOON SALTED CAPERS

2 SMALL GRELOT ONIONS

4 TEASPOONS UNSALTED BUTTER, MELTED

HANDFUL OF CORNES DE CERF (ROCKET LEAVES OR OAK LEAF LETTUCE CAN BE SUBSTITUTED FOR THIS DISTINCTIVE FRENCH LETTUCE)

$1/2$ LEMON

FLEUR DE SEL

FRESHLY GROUND PEPPER

FARMHOUSE JELLY WITH MACVIN

THIS DISH HAS ALL THE THINGS I LOVE: FIGS, SHERRY,

THE COMPLICITY BETWEEN SIMPLE FLAVORS LIKE VEGETABLE BOUILLON AND MACVIN.

1996

POMPADOUR POTATOES WITH ANDOUILLETTE DE VIRE STUFFING,
MACAU ARTICHOKE VELOUTÉ WITH TRUFFLES, GRILLED OYSTERS

Serves 4

STUFFED POTATOES

4 POMPADOUR POTATOES

1/8 POUND ANDOUILLETTE DE VIRE (CHITTERLING SAUSAGE), VERY THINLY SLICED

4 TEASPOONS UNSALTED BUTTER

ARTICHOKE VELOUTÉ

5 MACAU ARTICHOKES

1 GLASS WHITE WINE

PEEL OF 1 ORANGE

1 TEASPOON KOSHER SALT

SCANT CUP HEAVY CREAM, WARMED

ONE 1-OUNCE TRUFFLE (1/2 OUNCE CHOPPED, 1/2 OUNCE SLICED)

SCANT 1/2 CUP RED PORT, REDUCED BY THREE-QUARTERS

GRILLED OYSTERS

4 LARGE, FLESHY OYSTERS (SPÉCIALES NO.1)

2 TABLESPOONS FLOUR

1 EGG, BEATEN

3 TABLESPOONS FINELY GROUND BREAD CRUMBS

2 TABLESPOONS CLARIFIED UNSALTED BUTTER

STUFFED POTATOES

Wrap the potatoes in aluminum foil, place them in an earthenware dish, and bake for 40 minutes in an oven preheated to 350°F. Cut them in two and scoop out the insides, setting 4 of the 8 half-skins aside. Mash the flesh with a fork, and mix in the bits of *andouillette* and butter. Fill the 4 potato skins with this mixture.

ARTICHOKE VELOUTÉ

Place the artichoke hearts in a casserole and add 2 1/8 cups water, the white wine, orange peel, and salt. Cook for about 40 minutes, until they are done. (To check the progress of an artichoke heart, pierce the bottom; when it is tender, the artichoke is done.) Purée the hearts in a blender, add the heavy cream, chopped truffle, and reduced port.

At the last minute, thin the purée with a little of the stock you used for cooking the artichokes.

GRILLED OYSTERS

Roll the oysters in flour, coat with the beaten egg, and roll in the bread crumbs.

BEFORE SERVING

Heat the potatoes for 5 minutes in the oven. Sear the oysters for 2 minutes in the clarified butter, using a non-stick pan.

Pour a little artichoke velouté onto each plate. Lay a hot stuffed potato and a fried oyster onto the plate and cover with the truffle slices.

MONSIEUR CLOS'S POTATOES WERE THE INSPIRATION FOR THIS DISH.
I WANTED TO WORK WITH THOSE DELICIOUS PRODUCTS, TO DEVISE A MISE EN SCÈNE
WORTHY OF THEM. THE ANDOUILLETTE DE VIRE SLIPS RATHER WICKEDLY BETWEEN
THE POTATO AND THE OYSTER-BAKED POTATOES REVISITED.

Against Brutality

Pierre Gagnaire's restaurant on the rue de la Richelandière was a financial failure, and a brutal one. When the dust settled, nothing remained of all his efforts in the kitchen. Saint-Étienne had failed to respond. As much as the *stephanois* had loved Pierre's earlier restaurant, in a former photography studio on rue Georges-Tessier, they were unable to understand his new, larger-than-life restaurant on the rue de la Richelandière. This was regrettable, but in a town dedicated to soccer, occasional umpiring errors are part of the game.

The move to Paris didn't change Pierre's sensibility one iota. He never looked back, or even paused, and all his recipes remained inimitably his own. Yet they never quite took on his identity. He said so himself in his own lucid, slightly wistful way: "There's nothing on my bill of fare that identifies me, like *soupe aux truffes* identifies Bocuse, or *saumon à l'oseille* identifies Troisgros." But how could it be otherwise? For years Pierre wouldn't accept that there was such a thing as a "finished" recipe. Jacques Tati felt the same about his films. In a way, they were both right. The process of creation is one of continual adjustment.

From the start Pierre was against any approach to cuisine that was satisfied with the *mise-en-scène* of a single ingredient in all its "brutality," as he called it. The preface to his first book, *La cuisine immédiate* (1988), explained: "He has a tendency to soften food ingredients, coaxing them into a kind of social pact of *savoir-vivre*, wherein they encounter, flirt with, and even compromise themselves in the face of other ingredients that seem to be totally alien to them."

This may be the characteristic that best defines Pierre Gagnaire, both as a man and as a chef: a *savoir-vivre* that has no fixed rules, but functions within its own fluid sensibility. He was not embittered by the financial setback in Saint-Étienne. He called himself into question, confronting the facts without a trace of vanity. He remains just as sensitive to the reactions of people in his restaurants in the rue de Bac and rue Balzac as he was when he was a young chef on the threshold of his career. He has lived cuisine pretty much in the absolute—but not to the point where, as Aragon would say, it becomes a "wasting away of the soul" that makes a man's hands tremble as he works. Over the years, Pierre has learned to exercise a form of clairvoyance, and it has made his existence all the happier.

J.–F. A.

ARTICHOKE

NOT SO MUCH AN INDIVIDUAL ARTICHOKE AS ARTICHOKES IN GENERAL:

SPINY, MACAU, POIVRADE—AS YOU LIKE IT. HEARTS OF ARTICHOKE TAKE ME BACK TO MY CHILDHOOD.

A BEAUTIFUL, WELL-COOKED ARTICHOKE HEART, WITH A HINT OF CRUNCHINESS,

SERVED WITH A SLAB OF FOIE GRAS MAKES A MOST FESTIVE ENTRÉE.

MENU — JANUARY 1997

SABLÉ OF BLACK TRUFFLES
SWEET ONIONS, MARINADE OF GILLARDEAU OYSTERS AND YOUNG LEEKS

■

SPINY LOBSTER À LA NIORA
VELOUTÉ OF JERUSALEM ARTICHOKES, ROASTED GREEN ASPARAGUS

■

GREEN CABBAGE, BUFFALO MOZZARELLA, AND SEVRUGA CAVIAR
WITH EMULSIFIED CUCUMBER JUICE

■

JOHN DORY, SEA SCALLOPS, AND ESPARDEIGNES (SEA CUCUMBERS) SAUTÉED IN BROWN BUTTER
POT HERBS FLAVORED WITH URCHIN JUICE

■

POGGIGLIANO WHOLE BRAISED TURNIP
VEAL ESSENCE AND CHESTNUTS

■

SAUTÉED SLICE OF ROE DEER FILLET AU BERBERÉ
LIGHTLY CARAMELIZED PASTE OF MANGO AND GRAPEFRUIT

■

VINTAGE COMTÉ AND FRESH BOURGOGNE CHEESE
POMPADOUR, DATES, AND DRIED APRICOTS WITH FINO SHERRY

■

GRAND DESSERT PIERRE GAGNAIRE

GREEN CABBAGE, BUFFALO MOZZARELLA, AND SEVRUGA CAVIAR,
EMULSIFIED CUCUMBER JUICE

GREEN CABBAGE, MOZZARELLA, AND CAVIAR

Blanch the cabbage leaves for 2 minutes in a saucepan of boiling salted water. Drain, then cut them with a 1^1/$_4$-inch cutter and coat with butter. Slice the mozzarella balls, and cut the pike stuffing sausage into 1^1/$_4$-inch-thick rounds. Place a cabbage leaf and then a slice of mozzarella on each round of stuffing. Add a few drops of lemon juice and a little oil, and cover with another slice of cabbage leaf. Place the result in a small buttered baking dish and set aside in the refrigerator.

CUCUMBER JUICE

Peel the cucumber and cut into large cubes. Sprinkle these with fine salt and leave to drain excess water for half an hour.
Blend the cucumber flesh to make the juice, and incorporate the softened gelatin. Set aside in the refrigerator. Emulsify this cucumber jelly with the oil and milk; the texture should be quite creamy.

BEFORE SERVING

Place the discs of cabbage and mozzarella in an oven preheated to 325°F until they are just warm.
Pour the refrigerated emulsified cucumber juice onto cold plates; place the cabbage discs on top and lay a large spoonful of caviar on top of each.

Serves 4

GREEN CABBAGE, MOZZARELLA, AND CAVIAR

4 LEAVES OF ROUND, GREEN CABBAGE

1 TABLESPOON UNSALTED BUTTER

2 BALLS BUFFALO MOZZARELLA

1 SAUSAGE OF PIKE STUFFING (QUENELLE DE BROCHET), 1^1/$_4$ INCHES DIAMETER, POACHED

JUICE OF 1 LEMON

3^1/$_2$ TABLESPOONS OLIVE OIL

1 OUNCE SEVRUGA CAVIAR

CUCUMBER JUICE

1 EUROPEAN HOTHOUSE CUCUMBER

2 GELATIN LEAVES, SOFTENED IN COLD WATER

3^1/$_2$ TABLESPOONS OLIVE OIL

SCANT ^{1}/$_2$ CUP UNSALTED BUTTER

GREEN CABBAGE, BUFFALO MOZZARELLA, AND SEVRUGA CAVIAR

I CONCOCTED THIS DISH FOR ALAIN PASSARD, WHO WAS COMING TO CELEBRATE

THE AWARD OF HIS THIRD MICHELIN STAR THE FOLLOWING DAY.

I WAS LIVING THE LAST MONTHS OF MY SAINT-ÉTIENNE ADVENTURE. . .

PARIS
LE BALZAC

1 9 9 7

2 0 0 6

THE ADVENTURE CONTINUES IN PARIS
MENU — FEBRUARY 1997

SHREDDED BABY MACKEREL AND SCALLOPS DIPPED IN SALT
GREEN SEA URCHIN VELOUTÉ

BROTH OF MARINATED POIVRADE ARTICHOKES
CREAMY MOUSSELINE OF LAKE LÉMAN DACE

LOBSTER ROASTED WITH LEMONGRASS
SHANGHAI CABBAGE AND GREEN MANGO

POÊLÉE OF SHELLFISH AND CUTTLEFISH
SLOW-SMOKED FARMHOUSE PORK BELLY WITH PISTACHIO GRAVY

GRILLED NOISETTE OF SUCKLING LAMB
LAMB SWEETBREADS WITH SWEET ONIONS, CORNMEAL GALETTE WITH TRUFFLES

FARMHOUSE CHEESES

PIERRE GAGNAIRE'S DESSERTS

POÊLÉE OF SHELLFISH AND CUTTLEFISH,
SLOW-SMOKED FARMHOUSE PORK BELLY WITH PISTACHIO GRAVY

SHELLFISH POÊLÉE

Boil the white wine and the minced shallot in a large casserole. Add all the shellfish except the winkles and cook for 5 minutes with the lid on. Remove from heat and leave to cool, still covered. Remove the shells, strain the liquid very carefully, and reduce to 1/2 cup. Remove the cooked winkles from their shells and add them to the rest of the shellfish.

Brown the sliced cuttlefish in a nonstick frying pan with a little oil and the crushed garlic. Mix together the cuttlefish and shellfish in the shellfish cooking liquid, and add lemon juice and the chopped fresh herbs. Set aside.

PORK BELLY

To blanch the piece of pork belly, place it in a casserole of cold water, bring to a boil, and immediately drain. Using the same casserole, brown the onion and garlic in the oil. Place the belly on top, moisten with chicken stock, cover, and cook for 40 minutes over low heat.

Remove the meat from the casserole, pat it dry with paper towels, and place it on a rack. Put the rack in a heavy cast-iron pan, over a bed of hardwood shavings (oak or beech) and the aromatic herbs. Place the pot on the fire and heat until the shavings begin to smoke. Immediately remove the pot from the flame, cover, and smoke the meat for 30 minutes.

Remove the meat from the pan and set aside, keeping it warm under aluminum foil. At the last moment, cut the smoked meat into thick slices and grill them in a hot, nonstick frying pan.

PISTACHIO GRAVY

Reduce the cooking liquid from the pork to about 1 cup and stir in the pistachio paste, vinegar, and grapefruit juice. Strain through a *chinois* (a conical, fine-mesh strainer), sharpen with a little lemon juice, and add the roughly crushed pistachios.

BEFORE SERVING

Place a serving of shellfish in each heated soup plate, add a thick slice of hot crispy smoked pork belly, and coat with pistachio gravy. Garnish each plate with a few dandelion leaves tossed in the warm melted butter.

Serves 4

SHELLFISH POÊLÉE

1 1/2 POUNDS SHELLFISH (LITTLENECK CLAMS, VENUS CLAMS, COCKLES, COOKED WINKLES)

1/2 GLASS DRY WHITE WINE (CHARDONNAY)

1 SHALLOT, MINCED

5 1/2 OUNCES CUTTLEFISH, CLEANED AND PREPARED

3 1/2 TABLESPOONS OLIVE OIL

1 GARLIC CLOVE, CRUSHED

1/2 LEMON

1 TABLESPOON FRESH HERBS (FLAT-LEAF PARSLEY, YARROW), FINELY CHOPPED

PORK BELLY

1 3/4 POUNDS PORK BELLY

1 ONION, FINELY CHOPPED

2 GARLIC CLOVES, CRUSHED

1 TABLESPOON OLIVE OIL

1 2/3 CUPS CHICKEN STOCK (SEE PAGE 190)

THYME AND JUNIPER BERRIES

2 SPRIGS DRIED FENNEL

PISTACHIO GRAVY

1 TEASPOON UNSWEETENED PISTACHIO PASTE

3 1/2 TABLESPOONS RED WINE VINEGAR

1 SCANT CUP PINK GRAPEFRUIT JUICE

JUICE OF 1/2 LEMON

2 1/2 TABLESPOONS CRUSHED PISTACHIOS

HANDFUL OF DANDELION LEAVES

2 TABLESPOONS UNSALTED BUTTER, MELTED

TOMATOES

THESE DAYS, HOW MANY PEOPLE GET A CHANCE TO EAT A REALLY GOOD, IN-SEASON TOMATO?

THE TOMATO IS BOTH FRUIT AND VEGETABLE, AN EXQUISITELY SIMPLE THING.

SADLY, ALL TOO OFTEN IT IS BOTCHED AND TORTURED, AND ALL ITS QUALITIES ARE WASTED.

SICILIAN TOMATO PASTE WITH WHITE TUNA AND BLACK OLIVES,
POTATO QUENELLES WITH SQUID INK

Serves 4

TOMATO PASTE

6¹/₂ OUNCES WHITE TUNA OR BONITO

PINCH EACH OF COLOMBO (A SLIGHTLY BITTER SRI LANKAN CURRY MIXTURE), CURRY POWDER, PAPRIKA TANDOORI, AND ESPELETTE PEPPER

2 TEASPOONS GREEN PEPPERCORNS

3¹/₂ TABLESPOONS OLIVE OIL

2 VINE-RIPENED TOMATOES, PEELED, SEEDED, AND CHOPPED

3 GARLIC CLOVES

10 PITTED BLACK OLIVES

1 GLASS WHITE WINE (CHARDONNAY)

1 SPRIG ROSEMARY

SALT

1 TEASPOON SAVORA MUSTARD

SCANT ¹/₂ CUP LIQUID (FROM COCKLES OR MUSSELS COOKED À LA MARINIÈRE)

POTATO QUENELLES

3 POTATOES

COARSE SEA SALT

2 TABLESPOONS CORNSTARCH OR POTATO STARCH

1 EGG, BEATEN

1 SACHET SQUID INK

2¹/₈ CUPS PLUS 1 TABLESPOON CHICKEN STOCK (SEE PAGE 190)

1¹/₂ TABLESPOONS UNSALTED BUTTER

TOMATOES AND CROUTONS

2 TOMATOES

2 SLICES PLAIN WHITE BREAD

SCANT ¹/₂ CUP OLIVE OIL

TOMATO PASTE

Marinate the tuna in a dish with the spices (Colombo, curry, paprika, tandoori, Espelette pepper, and green peppercorns) and some of the olive oil. Cover with plastic wrap and set aside in the refrigerator for 2 hours. Pour the remaining oil into a casserole and brown the tuna in it. Add the tomatoes, garlic, olives, white wine, rosemary, and salt. Cook gently for 1¹/₂ hours. Set aside to cool.

Shred the tuna (discarding black parts, skin, and bones) and mix in a blender with the other cooking elements. Add the Savora mustard and the shellfish liquid to this mixture until you have a thickish paste. Set aside.

POTATO QUENELLES

Bake the potatoes in the oven for 45 minutes at 350°F, in their jackets, on a bed of coarse sea salt. Remove the cooked potato pulp and pass through a *tamis* (a fine-mesh, drum sieve). Add the cornstarch, beaten egg, and squid ink. Season the mash, then shape the quenelles and set them in a buttered baking dish.

TOMATOES AND CROUTONS

Cut the tomatoes in pieces, mash, and set them aside.

Dice the slices of bread into fairly small croutons, and brown them well in the oil. When they are golden, drain them on a paper towel.

BEFORE SERVING

Warm the potato quenelles in a tablespoon of chicken stock and a pat of butter. Place them on the hot plates, with a spoonful of tuna paste on a bed of mashed tomato beside them. Sprinkle with the croutons.

THIS IS A SUMMER DISH CONSTRUCTED IN A WINTER MODE:
A COMPOSITE OF TUNA, HEAVILY REDUCED AND VERY STRONG IN TASTE.

The Engine Room

Downstairs in the kitchen, the air is filled with the crash of pots, pans, and utensils, a constant percussive din that contrasts with the eerie silence of the *brigade* at work. In the kitchens at Sketch, nobody speaks except in terms of acquiescence. Discipline is the principal strength of the dishes produced here. There's no time for banter, for stargazing, or for discussing half-time scores. In the basement kitchen, London life begins to resemble life in the shadows—except that if you're working for Pierre Gagnaire, you know that your reward will be freedom from any lingering hint of amateurism.

There are a number of details, though, that are specific to Sketch. Here every chef's assistant and scullion sports a cap. The item is not, as one might imagine, a headpiece of bucolic English design, but a kind of white jockey's cap. "Much more practical than a chef's toque when you're ducking in and out of *garde-manger*," says a brisk cook from southwest France, who's here to complete his training.

Of course the language is part of that training: Mayfair should not be Babel. On the left, though, stands a Japanese who speaks no English but a little French. French is not banned, and though Sketch isn't precisely French-speaking, it's not really English-speaking either, nor is it an aggregate. When you hear one of these employees trying out his English, you think Maurice Chevalier deserved a doctorate. On the evening I was in Sketch's Gallery space, the *brigade* was under the command of an English chef, rapping out orders like a ship's captain. The cooks responded in unison, "Yes, Chef," as if they were saying, "Aye aye, Sir," and immediately you could feel the ship moving purposefully away from her berth. In the dining room above, the clients were unaware of the engines driving the evening forward, and nobody asked to see what was happening in the engine room. They just expected the food to appear, as they had every right to do.

It was ever thus: The upper deck has never cared to know what goes on below, and there's no gangway connecting them. Yet the voyage continues full speed ahead, and all is for the best.

J.–F. A.

MENU — DECEMBER 31, 1997
TAMERZA

Squab Jelly Gauthier with Ethiopian Mixed Spices
LEMON SHALLOT AND PRESERVED CALVILLE APPLE FLAVORED WITH CINNAMON

Velouté of Jerusalem Artichoke with Almond Milk
PASCALINE OF FRESH TRUFFLES

Roast Spiny Lobster with Salted Butter
COUSCOUS AU TABIL

Crumbly Sablé Shortbread with Dried Fruit and Foie Gras
SAFFRON APRICOT JUICE WITH POMEGRANATE

Open Bastilla of Eggplant and Tomatoes with Old Madeira Wine

Saddle of Suckling Lamb Grilled with Black Pepper and Cardamom
CUMIN-FLAVORED CARAMEL WAFER, SMALL SWEET PEPPER WITH PISTACHIO AND HAZELNUT STUFFING

Selected Sheep Cheeses
FRESH PERSIMMONS AND NUTMEG SQUASH PASTE

DESSERTS:
BLOOD ORANGE JELLY; PULP OF BLENDED WINTER FRUITS; GRAPEFRUIT MARMALADE WITH SILVER THYME; ICED ZABAGLIONE; TONKA BEANS, CARIBBEAN ICE CREAM; CRÈME PARESSEUSE WITH SAFFRON AND CRYSTALLIZED CRUNCHY PEANUTS; MOSCOVITE DE COCO FLAVORED WITH MADAGASCAR VANILLA, TAPIOCA MILK

On the plane, for the journey home:
CHESTNUT VELOUTÉ WITH TRUFFLES

CRUMBLY SABLÉ SHORTBREAD WITH DRIED FRUIT AND FOIE GRAS,
SAFFRON APRICOT SAUCE WITH POMEGRANATE

SABLÉ PASTRY

Mix together the flour and the butter, then add the sugar, pepper, salt, and lemon zest. Incorporate the egg, taking care not to work the dough too thoroughly. Roll it out between two sheets of wax paper and leave in the refrigerator for 30 minutes.

Cut 2-inch-wide rounds of pastry using a round cutter, and place them on a sheet of parchment paper. Slide this onto a baking tray and bake for 20 minutes or so in an oven preheated to 325°F; the cookies should come out dry and golden in color. Store them in an airtight tin.

APRICOT SAUCE

Heat the apricot pulp with the honey, taking care not to boil, then add the saffron and the eau-de-vie. Cover and leave to infuse for 15 minutes. Strain the pulp, which by now should be a beautiful amber color. Sharpen it with a squeeze of lemon juice and add pepper, then add the pomegranate seeds. Set aside.

DRIED FRUIT AND FOIE GRAS

Fry the foie gras scallops in a nonstick pan for 2 minutes on each side over high heat. Sauté the crushed walnuts and hazelnuts with the chopped figs, using some of the melted fat from the foie gras. Deglaze with the sweet wine and a few drops of lemon juice. Dice the foie gras scallops in 1/2-inch cubes and mix them with the fruit and nuts.

BEFORE SERVING

Spoon the foie gras and dried fruit and nut mixture onto warm plates and place a *sablé* on each one. Circle with apricot juice, sprinkle with the sugar-and-salt mixture, and serve.

Serves 4

SABLÉ PASTRY

2 CUPS ALL-PURPOSE FLOUR

1 CUP UNSALTED BUTTER

1 CUP SUGAR

PINCH OF GROUND PEPPER

PINCH OF SALT

GRATED ZEST OF 1 LEMON

1 EGG

APRICOT SAUCE

1 1/4 CUPS APRICOT PULP

1 TABLESPOON HONEY

4 SAFFRON STAMENS

2 TABLESPOONS APRICOT EAU-DE-VIE (NOYAUX DE POISSY)

JUICE OF 1/2 LEMON

PINCH OF GROUND BLACK PEPPER

2 TABLESPOONS FRESH POMEGRANATE SEEDS

MIXTURE OF 80 PERCENT POWDERED SUGAR AND 20 PERCENT FINE SALT

DRIED FRUIT AND FOIE GRAS

4 SCALLOPS OF FOIE GRAS

2 1/2 TABLESPOONS WALNUTS

2 1/2 TABLESPOONS HAZELNUTS

2 DRIED FIGS, CUT IN SMALL DICE

JUICE OF 1/2 LEMON

1 SCANT CUP SWEET WINE (CORSICAN MUSCATEL)

CRUMBLY SABLÉ SHORTBREAD
WITH DRIED FRUIT AND FOIE GRAS

THIS NEW YEAR'S EVE DISH WAS SERVED AT TAMERZA IN CONDITIONS THAT WERE ACROBATIC, TO PUT IT MILDLY.

EVERYTHING WAS FLOWN IN FROM PARIS: DECORATIONS, MUSICIANS, CROCKERY, EVEN THE RECIPE INGREDIENTS.

DINNER — JUNE 7, 1998

FILLET OF PEKIN DUCK BREAST WITH SWEET PEPPER OIL
CONFIT OF SHALLOTS AND TURNIPS FLAVORED WITH CINNAMON

▧

PIKE PERCH, BITTER ALMOND BLANCMANGE
MOUSSERON MUSHROOM BROTH

▧

UGLY FRUIT CRUMBLE
PRESSÉ OF TRUFFLES AND BABY ONIONS

▧

SHRIMP ASPIC WITH ROSEMARY
BOUQUET OF SPRING VEGETABLES WITH COW PARSLEY LEAVES, LOBSTER AU NATUREL WITH SALT CUISINÉ

▧

BREAST OF VEAL WITH OREGANO
GRILLED CHITTERLING SAUSAGE, SWISS CHARD AND CHANTERELLES WITH ALMONDS

▧

FEUILLETÉ OF ROQUEFORT CHEESE AND BEEFHEART TOMATOES

▧

PIERRE GAGNAIRE'S DESSERTS

UGLY FRUIT CRUMBLE,
PRESSÉ OF TRUFFLES AND BABY ONIONS

PRESSÉ OF TRUFFLES

Twenty-four hours in advance:

Brown the baby onions in a casserole with the butter and the pinch of sugar. When they are golden, add a glass of water and a pinch of salt and cook for 15 minutes (the juice should be reduced to a glaze that coats the baby onions).

Cut the onions in quarters. In a warm bowl, mix delicately the pieces of onion with the chopped truffle, vinegar, port, and veal glaze. Check the seasoning at this point; it should be subtle but quite spicy.

Place the preparation in four small square molds with rims, which you have previously lined with plastic wrap and a layer of sliced truffles. Leave for 24 hours in the refrigerator.

UGLY FRUIT CRUMBLE

Mix the flour with the dried fruit and nuts and the sugar. Incorporate the butter bit by bit. Roll out this preparation between two pieces of plastic wrap, freeze, and chop into pieces.

Split the ugly fruit quarters in half with a knife and lay them side by side in a baking dish. Pour the champagne over them, add the fresh butter in small pats, and cover with the crumble. Broil for 3–4 minutes, until the crumble is golden.

BEFORE SERVING

Steam the truffle *pressés* for a few minutes. Remove the plastic wrap and place the *pressés* on warm plates, with the crumble-covered ugly fruit quarters alongside.

Serves 4

PRESSÉ OF TRUFFLES

1 BUNCH WHITE BABY ONIONS (8 TO 10)

2 TEASPOONS UNSALTED BUTTER

PINCH OF SUGAR

ONE 1-OUNCE TRUFFLE (HALF CUT IN THIN SLICES, HALF FINELY CHOPPED)

1 TABLESPOON BALSAMIC VINEGAR

1 TABLESPOON RED PORT WINE

1 SCANT CUP HEAVILY REDUCED VEAL STOCK (GLACÉ DE VEAU)

SALT AND PEPPER

UGLY FRUIT CRUMBLE

²/₃ CUP FLOUR

¹/₃ CUP CHOPPED HAZELNUTS

¹/₃ CUP CHOPPED ALMONDS

¹/₂ CUP DEMERARA SUGAR

¹/₂ CUP PLUS 2 TEASPOONS UNSALTED BUTTER

1 UGLY FRUIT, CUT IN QUARTERS

1 SPLASH CHAMPAGNE

GRAPEFRUIT

"

THE GRAPEFRUIT IS A HIGHLY VERSATILE FRUIT THAT CAN ACCOMPANY ALL KINDS OF THINGS:

FISH, VEAL SWEETBREADS, DUCK, AND EVEN TRUFFLES. A REALLY GOOD GRAPEFRUIT IS TO MY TASTE MUCH MORE

INTERESTING THAN AN ORANGE OR A LEMON. IT HAS A GROWN-UP FLAVOR THAT IS BOTH SOUR AND SHARP.

"

Loyalty and Friendship

Pierre in the kitchen, Pierre on the phone, Pierre at a meeting—he is a protean figure. Time for him is like a thicket, which he clears away with his last-minute energy, cutting with great swipes of his machete. I am waiting for him at the bar at Le Balzac, and I have a novel to pass the time. Pierre's delays are a much greater incitement to read than any journey by train or plane.

I am waiting in comfort, you understand. A picture by Alechinsky hangs above the glass of Sancerre or Bourgogne Aligote that the loyal Claude has set before me. A dash of jazz plays around the tinkling ice cubes of the day's first cocktail. My thoughts wanders as I try to remember the name of the drummer on the recording.

It always seems to be raining in Paris when I go to Le Balzac, like in a Simenon novel. Today, the doors of the restaurant block out a melancholy, storm-beaten Champs-Elysées. At times like these, Pierre's establishment seems even more silent than usual, even more quilted and cozy. Its familiarity is comforting: an easy sensation to conjure up, once you delude yourself into thinking you know the place well. It's a bit like the first sentence of a novel that you are forever rereading. But has there been only one first sentence for Gagnaire?

The story, of course, didn't begin on the rue Balzac, but the "follies" of the rue de la Richlandière in Saint-Étienne finally seem to have achieved closure, as the psychoanalysts say. The décor here in Paris is much more studied: Pierre has passed from the baroque exuberance of Saint-Étienne to a much more economical classicism. It's not just the effect of the rain outside: Le Balzac really does have a softening effect on one's mood, even one's dreams. The Paris establishment was designed to show no trace of Pierre's lost gamble in Saint-Étienne.

Pierre's loyalties lie in another, more emotional place, and you can feel why he is loath to abandon his old friends. You chat with Claude, and then you look into the kitchen to say hello to Michel Nave, Pierre's second-in-command from time immemorial. Michel is a calm, sagacious chef who runs the ship with the steadiest of hands. There's no noise in his domain, never even the tinkle of a radio, nothing but immaculate efficiency.

That's the way it is. The image of Pierre Gagnaire is built on expectation and loyalty, or rather on loyalty buttressed by expectation. Now, quite unexpectedly, Pierre himself appears—flustered by his multiple activities, hustled along by the sheer energy of his life. He is dressed half in chef's uniform and half in ordinary clothes. His arrival is so sudden you actually wonder if you got the date wrong. Not at all: Although Pierre can be a trifle fuzzy over a quasi-military summons to a "meeting," he never forgets a rendezvous with a friend. He will always appear; even when you've given up on him, he will eventually materialize out of nowhere, passing through walls of solid stone to reach you. With him, friendship is non-negotiable, a living thing, always immediate, always open-hearted, even though it seems to have evolved along with his professional experience. Against all the caprices of fortune and time, friendship for him marks the continuity of the years as they pass. He looks to his friendships as the logical explanation of his progress from Saint-Priest-en-Jarez to Paris. He is right: Friendship in the absolute has all the virtues of a good traveling companion.

Pierre's friendships have given him the ability to find himself in his cuisine, his aesthetic, and his tastes. They have provided the distance that his enthusiasm has required, whether or not he was aware of it. Over the years, they have provided him with a kind of impartiality, of the type that newspaper editors have. There is an analogy here to the figure Chapel used to call the "client'ami," someone who comes to your establishment often enough to really know it, and who therefore has the authority to disapprove of a dish that might be alien to its nature; someone who can bring a modicum of objectivity to the fits and starts of an impetuously subjective creator.

Pierre's greatest talent is that he has brought about a triumph of subjectivity in a world of that was dangerously standardized if not completely hermetic. He may not have exactly revolutionized the language of cuisine, but he has certainly invented and imposed a terminology and syntax of his own. Many of the younger generation of chefs, including those who forget to give credit where credit is due, have Pierre to thank for their freedom to approach cuisine without inhibition.

J.–F. A.

CAILLETTE OF KID WITH SORREL,
BABY FENNEL AND MONTPELLIER ROUGETTE, CARROT ESSENCE WITH ARGAN OIL, ALMOND CAKE AND ROCAMADOUR CHEESE

Serves 6

CAILLETTE

²/₃ POUND BONED KID (INCLUDING KIDNEYS)

1 GLASS WHITE WINE (CHARDONNAY)

3 TABLESPOONS OLIVE OIL

3 SPRIGS LEMON THYME

2 OUNCES MUSHROOMS

2 GARLIC CLOVES

HANDFUL OF PARSLEY STEMS

1 BUNCH SORREL

1½ TABLESPOONS UNSALTED BUTTER

2½ OUNCES PORK NECK (FAT)

4½ OUNCES PORK NECK (LEAN)

2 SLICES DRIED WHITE BREAD

2½ TABLESPOONS MILK

1 EGG, BEATEN

1 TEASPOON HONEY

SALT AND PEPPER

1⅛ POUNDS PIG'S CAUL (WELL SOAKED AND CLEANED IN COLD WATER)

4 TEASPOONS CLARIFIED UNSALTED BUTTER

3½ TABLESPOONS ORLÉANS VINEGAR

1 SCANT CUP HEAVY CREAM

FENNEL AND ROUGETTE

1¼ CUPS MINERAL WATER

¼ CUP SUGAR

1¼ CUPS VINEGAR

1 STAR ANISE POD

1 FENNEL BULB

2 ROUGETTE DE MONTPELLIER SALAD LEAVES

CAILLETTE

Twenty-four hours in advance:

Marinate the goat meat, cut in fairly substantial pieces, with the white wine, oil, lemon thyme, chopped mushrooms, crushed garlic, and parsley stems.

The next day:

Remove the sorrel stalks, heat the leaves in a pan with a pat of butter, and set aside to cool.

Drain the goat meat, reserving the marinade. Mince the meat along with the flesh and fat from the pig's neck and the white bread, soaked in milk. Add the sorrel, then the beaten egg. Season this mixture with honey, salt, and pepper. Cut out 6 squares of pig's caul and apportion the mixture in equal parts to each square, and fold into small disc-like bundles.

Now heat the clarified butter and a little oil in an ovenproof cassesrole. Put the bundles in with their folded sides down. Cook in an oven preheated to 350°F for 20–25 minutes to roast the *caillettes,* basting them regularly. Set aside in the same casserole until cool. Remove them and discard the cooking fat. Put the casserole back on the heat and use it to heat the vegetables from the marinade. When these become golden, deglaze with the vinegar and reduce by three-quarters. Add the cream and simmer for 5 minutes. Season, and strain the sauce. Set aside and keep warm.

FENNEL AND ROUGETTE

Bring the mineral water to a boil with the sugar and the vinegar. Infuse the star anise in this hot syrup.

Cut out the layers of fennel one by one, and blanch them for 5 minutes in a saucepan of boiling salted water. Drain and plunge them into the hot syrup, leaving them to stew for 40 minutes over very low heat. Drain again, very carefully.

Plunge the *rougette* salad leaves into the hot syrup for a few minutes only. Drain very carefully.

CAILLETTE OF KID WITH SORREL

CARROT ESSENCE

Reduce the carrot juice by half. Emulsify in a blender, adding the two oils. Season and set aside at room temperature.

ALMOND CAKE

Mix the powdered almonds, flour, yeast, and salt and pass through a *tamis* (a fine-mesh, drum sieve). Place this mixture in a large bowl, and incorporate the milk, almond paste, honey, and half the egg whites. When the mixture is smooth, add the remaining egg whites, the toasted chopped almonds, and the butter. Stir this preparation until it is completely blended.

Spoon the mixture into small nonstick cake molds 3¼ inches in diameter and bake for 6 minutes in an oven preheated to 375°F. Turn the cakes out of the molds and leave on a rack to cool.

BEFORE SERVING

Place a Rocamadour cheese on each cake and slip them into a hot oven (350°F) for about 30 seconds. Arrange the fennel and *rougette* leaves in the middle of warmed plates. Then place a *caillette* on top, with a cake beside it. Trace a line of emulsified carrot essence around each plate. Serve the cream sauce separately.

IT IS SCARCELY POSSIBLE TO IMPROVE ON A DELICIOUS PRODUCT
HANDLED SIMPLY AND WELL: WHAT COULD BE BETTER THAN A WELL-ROASTED,
WELL-GRILLED HAUNCH OF SUCKLING KID, SERVED IN SLICES? BUT SINCE EVEN
THE BEST CUTS OF KID ARE HARDLY COPIOUS, I WORKED UP THIS RECIPE
AS A WAY OF PUTTING THE REST OF THE MEAT TO GOOD USE.

CARROT ESSENCE

1⅔ CUPS CARROT JUICE

½ TABLESPOON ARGAN OIL

2 TABLESPOONS OLIVE OIL

ALMOND CAKE

¾ CUP ALMOND FLOUR

1 SCANT CUP ALL-PURPOSE FLOUR

⅜ OUNCE POWDERED YEAST

2½ TEASPOONS SALT

3½ TABLESPOONS MILK

2 TABLESPOONS ALMOND PASTE

1 TABLESPOON HONEY

1 CUP EGG WHITES (ABOUT 7)

⅓ CUP TOASTED CHOPPED ALMONDS

1 SCANT CUP MELTED UNSALTED BUTTER

6 RIPE ROCAMADOUR CHEESES

SALT AND PEPPER

MENU — SPRING 1999

CHAUD-FROID OF BRETON LANGOUSTINES
CARAMEL OF ALMONDS WITH FRESH SWEETCORN GRAINS

RED TUNA AND RED MULLET JELLY WITH NYONS OLIVES
POMPADOUR POTATO AND FOIE GRAS WITH ESPELETTE PEPPER

BISCUIT OF LOCAL PIKE
PAN-FRIED FROG LEGS WITH NEW GARLIC, WHITE ASPARAGUS JUICE WITH MALAGUETTA PEPPER

"JARDIN DE CURÉ" ROMAINE LEAVES
VELOUTÉ OF GRILLED PUMPKIN WITH RAPESEED OIL

ROASTED SEA BASS
EINKORN WITH FRESH HAM, EMULSIFIED CREAMED OYSTER JUICE

VEAL STEAK SIMMERED WITH CITRUS FRUITS
GRATIN OF SWEET SAINT-ANDRÉ ONIONS, BEEFHEART CABBAGE, AND "TERRE DE SIENNE" CLOCHARD APPLE

FARMHOUSE CHEESES

PIERRE GAGNAIRE'S DESSERTS

"JARDIN DU CURÉ" ROMAINE LEAVES,
VELOUTÉ OF GRILLED PUMPKIN WITH RAPESEED OIL

PUMPKIN VELOUTÉ

Sauté the pumpkin quarters in the butter, then add the star anise, sugar, vinegar, and tomato paste. Incorporate the banana rounds, simmer for a few minutes, and moisten with the milk and a little water. Salt lightly, add the bouquet garni, and cook for 25 minutes over low heat. Remove the bouquet garni and the star anise. Blend, then pass the resultant velouté through a *tamis* (a fine-mesh, drum sieve).

At the last minute add a little whipped cream and some chicken stock, then blend again so the velouté is foamy.

ROMAINE LEAVES

Boil 3 tablespoons of water with the butter, tarragon leaves, and a pinch of salt. Plunge the romaine leaves in this for 2 minutes and drain immediately.

Warm the Swiss chard, turnips, cherry tomatoes, and radishes in the romaine leaves' cooking juices. Roll the carrots, with their tops, in a little mustard-flavored chicken stock.

Cut the baby squash in two lengthwise and cook them, tossing, in a frying pan with a little hot oil for 1 minute. All the vegetables should be barely cooked—crunchy and full of vivacity and freshness. Arrange them attractively on the romaine leaves.

BEFORE SERVING

Cut the surface of the velouté with a line of rapeseed oil and pour it into hot soup plates; then top with some of the romaine leaves and some of each of the baby vegetables.

Serves 4

PUMPKIN VELOUTÉ

1 1/8 POUNDS PUMPKIN, PEELED, SEEDED, AND CUT IN QUARTERS

1 TABLESPOON UNSALTED BUTTER

1 PETAL STAR ANISE

PINCH OF SUGAR

2 TABLESPOONS VINEGAR

1/2 TEASPOON TOMATO PASTE

1/2 BANANA, CUT INTO ROUNDS

2/3 CUP MILK

1 BOUQUET GARNI (PARSLEY, THYME, AND BAY LEAF, TIED WITH A LEEK)

1 SCANT CUP HEAVY CREAM, WHIPPED

1 SCANT CUP CHICKEN STOCK (SEE PAGE 190)

RAPESEED OIL

ROMAINE LEAVES

4 THICK ROMAINE LEAVES

1 TABLESPOON UNSALTED BUTTER

2 SPRIGS TARRAGON

PINCH OF SALT

SCANT 1/2 CUP CHICKEN STOCK

1 TEASPOON MUSTARD

BABY VEGETABLES IN SEASON: COOKED SWISS CHARD STALKS, SLIGHTLY STEAMED CARROTS, TURNIPS, AND CHERRY TOMATOES WITH THEIR STEMS, VERY SLIGHTLY BLANCHED RADISHES, BABY SQUASH

1 TABLESPOON OLIVE OIL

BLACK RICE

I DON'T THINK COOKS HAVE ADEQUATELY EXPLORED TEXTURE. OUR PERCEPTION OF FOOD IS GREATLY

INFLUENCED BY TEXTURE. BLACK RICE, FOR EXAMPLE, HAS A DISTINCTIVE SMOOTHNESS ALL ITS OWN.

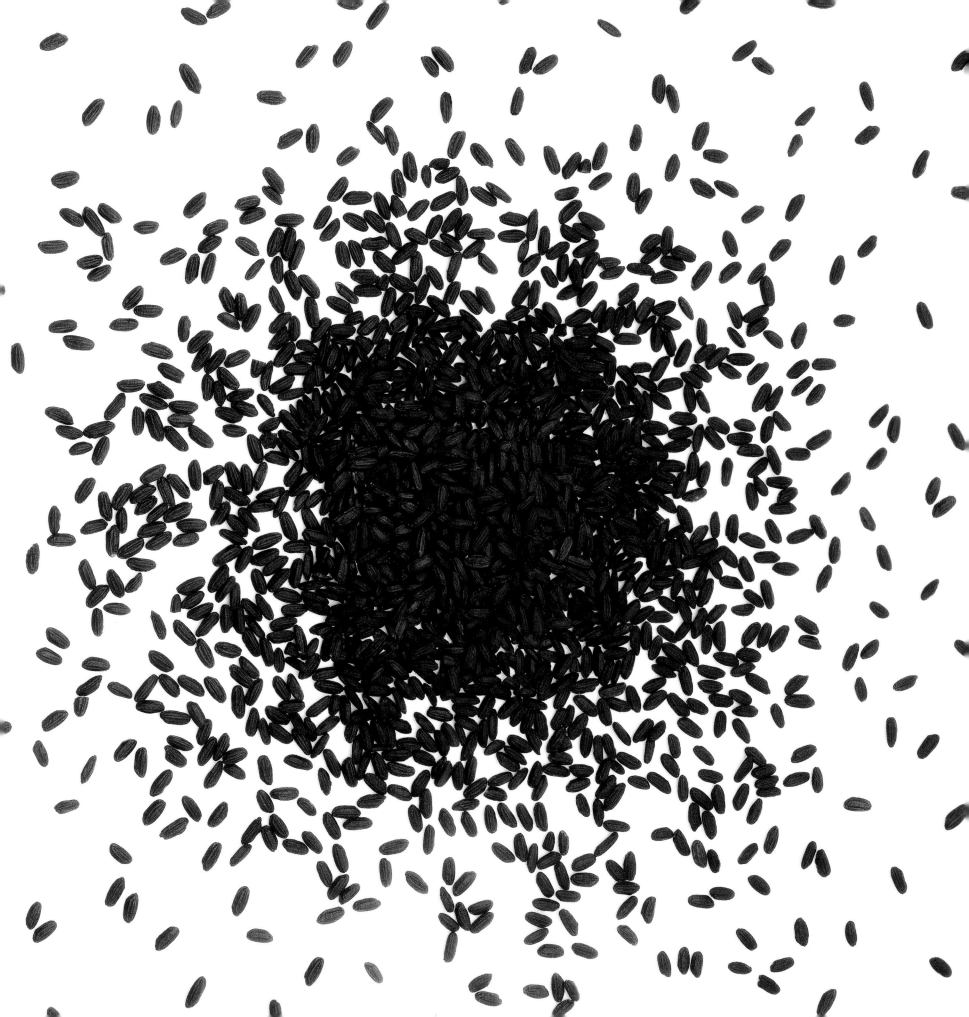

COCOTTE OF GILLARDEAU OYSTERS WITH SEAWEED,

DUCK FOIE GRAS POACHED À LA FICELLE IN ARTICHOKE AND CIDER STOCK,
ANCHOVY PURÉE AND CRUNCHY BABY VEGETABLES WITH CHURIZEROS PEPPER

Serves 4

ARTICHOKE STOCK

4 ARTICHOKES

1 QUART MINERAL WATER

HANDFUL OF PARSLEY STEMS

GENEROUS PINCH OF COARSE SEA SALT

1 GLASS FARMHOUSE CIDER

**ANCHOVY PURÉE AND
CRUNCHY VEGETABLES**

FRESH BABY VEGETABLES:
CARROTS, BROCCOLI AND
CAULIFLOWER FLORETS, SQUASH

1 CHURIZEROS PEPPER

3 1/2 OUNCES PITTED BLACK OLIVES

4 ANCHOVY FILLETS, PRESERVED IN OIL

2 TABLESPOONS OLIVE OIL

ARTICHOKE STOCK

Break off the stems of the artichokes, strip the leaves, and place all these in a large stainless steel casserole. Pour in the mineral water, add the parsley stems and a good pinch of coarse sea salt, and cook for 40 minutes over medium heat. Leave for 1 hour, strain the stock, and set aside. Discard everything except the artichoke hearts; pass the hearts through a *tamis* (a fine-mesh, drum sieve). Set aside the resultant purée at room temperature in a small covered container.

ANCHOVY PURÉE AND CRUNCHY VEGETABLES

Blanch the baby vegetables for a few minutes in a pot of boiling salted water, immediately cool them off in a bowl of iced water (to preserve their crunchy texture), and strain. Open up the hot pepper and carefully remove all the seeds.
Blend the pitted black olives with the anchovy fillets and the flesh of the pepper. Incorporate the oil drop by drop until you have a thick purée. Set aside in a container in the refrigerator.

FOIE GRAS À LA FICELLE

Wrap each slice of foie gras in a blanched green cabbage leaf. Tie each bundle with kitchen string to hold it together, leaving a 12-inch length of string dangling off. Pour off 1 1/4 cups of artichoke stock, blend it with 2 tablespoons of artichoke purée and a substantial pat of butter.
At the last minute, reheat the rest of the artichoke stock with the cider. Check the seasoning, and pour the mixture into your best copper saucepan. Lower the cabbage-wrapped foie gras packets by their strings into the simmering stock and poach for 4 minutes only.

OYSTER COCOTTE

Open the oysters and strain their liquid into a bowl.

Butter a small *cocotte* (an enamel or copper casserole or casserole dish). Sprinkle the shallots and the seaweed in the bottom. Add the oysters and pour the white wine over them. Place the *cocotte* in an oven preheated to 425°F and bake for 5 minutes.

BEFORE SERVING

Bring the *cocotte* of oysters and the saucepan containing the foie gras to the dinner table, with everybody seated round it. Serve 5 oysters per plate.

Remove the foie gras packets from the casserole, remove the string, and sprinkle with fleur de sel and freshly ground black pepper. Place the foie gras on the oysters, pour over a little artichoke stock, and apply a band of creamed artichoke purée.

FOIE GRAS À LA FICELLE

4 THICK SLICES OF FRESH DUCK FOIE GRAS (ABOUT 3 OUNCES EACH)

4 LEAVES GREEN CABBAGE, BLANCHED

1 TABLESPOON UNSALTED BUTTER

COCOTTE OF OYSTERS

20 OYSTERS (SPÉCIALES NO. 2)

1 1/2 TABLESPOONS UNSALTED BUTTER

2 SHALLOTS, FINELY CHOPPED

1 TABLESPOON DRIED SEAWEED FLAKES (DULSE OR SEA LETTUCE)

1/2 GLASS WHITE WINE (CHARDONNAY)

FLEUR DE SEL MIXED WITH A TOUCH OF PEANUT OIL

BLACK PEPPER, MIGNONNETTE

COCOTTE OF OYSTERS AND DUCK FOIE GRAS
POACHED À LA FICELLE

"

THERE ARE THREE IDEAS BEHIND THIS DISH: OYSTERS FOR THE TANG OF THE SEA,

FOIE GRAS FOR A RICH, MELTING QUALITY, AND ARTICHOKE FOR ITS BITTERNESS WHEN COMBINED

WITH THE TASTE OF APPLE CIDER. GENERALLY THE ARTICHOKE HAS A CERTAIN ELEGANCE TO MATCH

ITS SAVOR AND ITS ABILITY TO BIND; BUT ALL TOO OFTEN IT LACKS AN ADEQUATE FOIL TO GIVE IT REAL PANACHE.

"

Impressions of Sketch

S ketch has nothing to do with conventional good manners. Nor does taste enter into the equation, though tastes very much do. The style of the building includes the same emulsions and color blends that Gagnaire's kitchen produces. Confronted by the stream of contemporary art films and videos (the day we were there, a Jonas Mekas retrospective was showing), the crypto-futuristic decorative elements (small egg-shaped kiosks), and the flurry of electric grooves—combined with the elegance of Gagnaire's cuisine (or rather the cuisine of his chef, Pascal Sanchez)—well, a few English commentators have lost their cool. Sketch has been called a "museum of horrors," and given a rating of 0 out of 20 by British magazines rendered hysterical by the restaurant's violation of Mayfair. This most chic of London areas would never recover, claimed the naysayers, concluding that Sketch was the biggest disaster Britain had endured since the Channel Tunnel. "Nobody seemed to notice that we restored a ruined building," says Mourad Mazouz, Sketch's co-creator.

But there's nothing like apocalyptic commentary for attracting energy. As it turns out, the neighborhood was given a shot in the arm, a new lease on life. Sketch has several floors (including the Lecture Room and Library, the Gallery, and the Parlour), with nothing in common but Gagnaire's cuisine. Not too far from Carnaby Street, Sketch is treasured for its youthful insolence and playful, goofy provocation. You can sense its magnetic power; indeed, you find yourself glued to your table as if you were watching a play directed by Peter Sellars.

Mourad, with his artistic projects, indefatigable curiosity, and headlong pace, heightens this sense of energy through the recordings he makes for Sketch, and through the diversity of new elements he constantly injects into the building. The whole structure of Sketch seems to flow along the natural curve of a kitchen that refuses to repeat the same dishes for two days running. Along with Mourad, there is Sinead Mallozzi, who administers the premises with implacable sang-froid. The daughter of a golf professional, she is methodical and orderly to a very high degree.

Having been caught frequently between the rock of creativity and the hard place of economic realism, Pierre Gagnaire seems perfectly qualified to mediate between the two poles. He performs the task with the courtesy, civility, and professionalism we would expect of him. He leaves nothing unattended—except perhaps his own briefcase, which he has been known to do just before boarding the Eurostar.

140

It is possible to approach Sketch from another angle altogether. As its name implies, it is conceived as a drawing, an outline—not a painting meant to last forever. "It is," writes Gagnaire, "a project repeatedly corrected and a story constantly rewritten." Sketch is caught up in a current that has the power to alter its destiny at any time. Depending on the hour, the tearoom at Sketch may metamorphose into an aperitif room, an impromptu snack bar, or a concert hall. Mourad Mazouz remains a nomad in a city that has a much more sedentary idea of its own history, or rather a more fixed sense of its price, than he has.

Mayfair is London's gallery area, where you can buy paintings by Pissarro, drawings by Derain or Henry Moore, and sculptures by Barry Flanagan (though the prices are enough to make your hair stand on end). In the plush world of Mayfair, polished by centuries of soft manners and money, Sketch is monumentally incongruous and out of place. This is what makes it successful, and gives it the catalytic quality characteristic of fashion trends and counter trends. An odd destiny, but an interesting one.

J.–F. A.

JODHPUR SEA BASS EN PAPILLOTE,
NIORA PEPPER PASTE AND ALMOND CREAM, RED CAMARGUE RICE, MEDJOOL DATES, AND BABY ONIONS, INFUSION OF CÈPES WITH SCORCHED TOAST, TAMBA KOURA MAME AND GLAZED SHALLOTS

Serves 4

INFUSION OF CÈPES

5½ OUNCES DRIED CÈPES

SCANT ½ CUP VEGETABLE STOCK

1 SLICE OF WELL-GRILLED, ALMOST BURNED BREAD (ABOUT 1½ OUNCES), BROKEN INTO PIECES

TAMBA KOURO MAME AND SHALLOTS

⅛ POUND DRIED TAMBA KOURO MAME BEANS*

1 ONION, STUDDED WITH CLOVES

1 BOUQUET GARNI (PARSLEY, THYME, AND BAY LEAF, TIED WITH A LEEK)

4 SHALLOTS, PEELED

1 BAY LEAF

1 TABLESPOON CLARIFIED UNSALTED BUTTER

PINCH OF SUGAR

PINCH OF SALT

FRESH CÈPES

⅓ POUND FRESH CÈPES, FINELY CHOPPED

SPLASH OF OLIVE OIL

1 TABLESPOON UNSALTED BUTTER

1 GARLIC CLOVE

1 TEASPOON BREAD CRUMBS

ALMOND CREAM

3½ TABLESPOONS HEAVY CREAM

3½ TABLESPOONS CHICKEN STOCK (SEE PAGE 190)

1 TEASPOON ALMOND PASTE

* TAMBA KOURO MAME BEANS ARE DRIED BLACK BEANS OF VARIOUS SIZES; IN JAPAN THEY ARE CONSIDERED TO BE THE BEST DRIED VEGETABLE AVAILABLE.

INFUSION OF CÈPES

The day before:
Infuse the dried cèpes overnight in the vegetable stock.
The next day:
Bring the stock to a boil with the cèpes and simmer for 2 hours. Add the broken-up scorched toast, bring back to a boil, season, and strain. Set aside and keep warm.

TAMBA KOURO MAME

The day before:
Put the dried beans to soak overnight in a large bowl of cold water.
The next day:
Strain the beans, place them in a casserole with the clove-studded onion and the bouquet garni, cover with spring water, and cook over the lowest heat possible; the cooking must be extremely gentle or the beans will burst. Salt only when cooking has been completed.

SHALLOTS

Place the shallots in a casserole with the bay leaf and clarified butter and cook until golden. Add the pinch of sugar and a pinch of salt and cook for a further 35–40 minutes, moistening with a little water. The juice will reduce and coat the shallots with a thin caramelized glaze. Set aside.

FRESH CÈPES

Sauté the chopped cèpes in the butter and oil. Season with salt and add the crushed garlic and bread crumbs. Set aside and keep warm.

ALMOND CREAM

Reduce the heavy cream to a minimum over low heat, then add the chicken stock and almond paste; the resultant cream should be thick enough to coat a spoon). Salt lightly, set aside, and keep warm.

RICE AND DATES

Cook the rice like a pilaf, with the onion. This type of rice takes a long time to cook, at least 50 minutes. Open the dates, stuff them with the cooked rice and set them aside in the chicken stock to keep them warm.

JODHPUR SEA BASS EN PAPILLOTE

JODHPUR SEA BASS

Remove the backbone of the sea bass by cutting it open at the back. Then remove all the little bones along the flanks using tweezers.

Spread a large piece of parchment paper on a work surface and sprinkle it with the Jodhpur spices. Cover the spices with the rounds of potato, and place the fish on top of the bed of potatoes, along with the orange and lemon peel. Sprinkle with the stock, sherry, and port. Dot the fish all over with small pats of butter and sprinkle with fleur de sel. Now enclose the fish in the paper by folding and pinching it into a tight and secure envelope (papillote) and place it on a baking tray. (The fish should be resting on the potatoes so it doesn't have contact with the baking tray, but cooks in the spicy vapor of the stock instead. Likewise, the spices are underneath the potato rounds, not sprinkled over the fish, which preserves its delicate taste.) Cook in an oven preheated to 425°F for 5 minutes only.

Open the papillote in the presence of the guests, presenting the fish to the guests and letting them enjoy its beauty and wonderful aromas, then take it back to the kitchen. Pour the cooking juices out of the papillote into a pan. Lay the two fillets skin down in the juice and cook for a further 5 minutes over low heat, basting constantly. (Basting is as vital for fish as for meat; basting enriches, nourishes, and perfumes the flesh, and keeps it from drying out.) Set aside the fillets in a dish and keep warm, covered with aluminum foil.

Bring the cooking juices to a rapid boil; they will turn into a foamy, buttery sauce. Correct the seasoning with pepper, salt, and a drop of lemon juice and strain through a sieve, pressing as hard as you can. Set aside and keep warm.

BEFORE SERVING

Place a little niora pepper paste in each of your four heated plates, then carefully place the sea bass fillets over it. Apportion the cèpes, pouring some almond cream over them. Place a tablespoon of beans and a glazed shallot in each of four small bowls and, at the table in front of your guests, pour the piping hot cèpe infusion into each bowl.

At the last minute, coat the fish with the foamy, buttery sauce.

Serve the dates and rice separately, on a small dish.

THE INSPIRATION FOR THIS DISH WAS TRAVEL TO A DISTANT LAND, ON ANOTHER CONTINENT. ONE DAY I RECEIVED A PACKAGE OF SPICES FROM AN INDIAN IN JODHPUR. I SPONTANEOUSLY USED THEM WITH A FISH—LIKE THIS, COOKED EN PAPILLOTE. THE FISH COOKS IN ITS OWN JUICE; AND THE JUICE ITSELF TURNS INTO A CONCENTRATED BUTTER, GROWING STRONGER AND MORE DENSE UNTIL IT IS ALMOST SOUR.

RICE AND DATES

1/8 POUND (3 OUNCES) RED RICE

1 ONION

8 MEDJOOL DATES

1 SCANT CUP CHICKEN STOCK

SALT AND PEPPER

JODHPUR SEA BASS

1 SEA BASS (ABOUT 1³/₄ POUNDS)

1 TEASPOON MIXED SPICES FROM JODHPUR (SEE PAGE 195)

3 SLICES OF POTATO, CUT 1 INCH THICK

PEEL OF 1 LEMON

PEEL OF 1 ORANGE

3¹/₂ TABLESPOONS CHICKEN STOCK

1 TABLESPOON AMONTILLADO SHERRY

1 TABLESPOON WHITE PORT

2 TABLESPOONS UNSALTED BUTTER

1/2 LEMON

FLEUR DE SEL

1 TEASPOON NIORA PEPPER PASTE (SEE PAGE 195)

SEA URCHIN CORALS,

CUTTLEFISH SHAVINGS, ASPARAGUS TIPS WITH CAVIAR, EGG YOLKS MACASSAR

Serves 4

CUTTLEFISH SHAVINGS

1/2 BUNCH WATERCRESS

FLESH OF 1 CUTTLEFISH, VERY THICK

1 TABLESPOON SALTED SEAWEED FLAKES

EGG YOLKS MACASSAR

4 EGGS

1 OUNCE TRUFFLES, CHOPPED

2 TABLESPOONS FRESH BREAD CRUMBS

1 TABLESPOON MELTED UNSALTED BUTTER

SCANT 1/2 CUP PORT WINE, REDUCED
UNTIL SYRUPY (ABOUT 2 TABLESPOONS)

SEA URCHINS

8 SEA URCHINS

1 1/2 TABLESPOONS UNSALTED BUTTER,
COOKED UNTIL IT IS GOLDEN BROWN AND
HAS A NUTTY AROMA (BEURRE NOISETTE)

1 TABLESPOON OLIVE OIL

2 GLASSES WHITE WINE (CHARDONNAY)

1 SCANT CUP HEAVY CREAM

CUTTLEFISH SHAVINGS

Remove the watercress leaves from the stems, blanch for a few seconds in boiling water, cool immediately under cold running water, and drain carefully. Set aside.

Sear the cuttlefish flesh very quickly in a nonstick pan without fat; it should be golden, but still almost raw. Wrap it in plastic wrap and place it in the freezer.

Just before serving, shave off thin flakes of the frozen flesh with a cheese parer and mix them with the blanched watercress leaves and seaweed.

EGG YOLKS MACASSAR

Soft-boil the eggs (cook 8 minutes in boiling water), cool under cold running water, and peel off the shells. The yolks should be just cooked enough not to run.

Mix the chopped truffles, bread crumbs, melted butter, and port. With the utmost care, roll the egg yolks in this mixture (they must not crumble), and set them aside on a dish.

SEA URCHINS AND CRÈME D'OURSINS

Open the sea urchins, reserving and straining their liquid. Set aside the shells to make the *crème d'oursins.* Detach the corals and place them in the strained juice. Set aside in the refrigerator.

At the last minute, lay the corals in a small dish with 2 tablespoons of their juice. Pour on the *beurre noisette* and mix with extreme care.

Crush the urchin shells well and sauté them in the oil. Moisten with the white wine and 3 glasses of water and simmer for 30 minutes. Cool, strain, and reduce the juice with the cream added, until you have a smooth sauce. Season with salt and pepper and set aside to cool.

ASPARAGUS TIPS

Tie the asparagus into a bunch and blanch for 5 minutes in a pan of boiling salted water. Immediately plunge them into a bowl of iced water, then drain carefully on kitchen towels. Chop off the tips at about the 6-inch mark, keeping the lower, discarded halves for some other use. At the last minute, warm the tips and slice them in two, lengthwise.

BEFORE SERVING

Using soup plates, arrange the ingredients in this order: a little hot sauerkraut, the flakes of cuttlefish with the watercress leaves, and the sea urchin corals. Distribute the asparagus spears among the soup plates and drop a few caviar eggs on each tip. Coat each portion with the cooking butter from the sea urchin corals. Pour the cold sea urchin cream into separate plates, with a Macassar egg yolk in the center of each.

SEA URCHIN CORAL IS A RARE AND VERY DEMANDING ITEM;
INDEED, IT IS A REAL DISCOVERY, RAW YET PERFECTLY CIVILIZED.
I LOVE THIS DISH—IMAGINE EATING FIVE OR SIX URCHIN CORALS, BARELY WARM IN
THEIR BEURRE NOISETTE, WITH THE RICH FAT SURROUNDING AND MAGNIFYING
THEIR SUMPTUOUS ELEGANCE AND SEA ORIGIN.

ASPARAGUS TIPS

8 STALKS ASPARAGUS

1 OUNCE CAVIAR

$1/2$ CUP COOKED SAUERKRAUT

SALT AND PEPPER

Wine and Silence

Pierre Gagnaire admires the vitality of people who make wine. He especially likes the way they respond to sudden emergencies like hailstorms.

From time to time he invites winemakers to partake in his cooking, just as Alain Chapel used to do. Some of them belong to the winemakers' union, an association in France that has no political objectives but exists only to promote friendships among the *vigneron* fraternity. Its network of solidarity stretches from Meursault (Jean-Marc Roulot) to Pont-de-l'Isère (Alain Graillot and his Crozes-Hermitages). When these comrades in wine get together, usually in the establishments of France's best chefs, the bottles clash merrily; the tribe of *vignerons* actively dislikes all constraints. As you might imagine, this category includes anything resembling a flask, a half bottle, or a half-empty glass, all of which can lower a man's spirits.

Pierre himself is a very moderate drinker. Perhaps in the back of his mind he remembers the chefs of the Third and Fourth Republics, who drank alcohol to combat the heat of their ovens. (Today they would be fighting the heat of spotlights, but in those times, cooks spent their time in sculleries, not television studios.) Raymond Oliver and Paul Bocuse changed all that, but before them there was a lost generation of prodigally gifted chefs in France, who straddled the chasm between old and new.

I can provide one melancholy example: One day I went with Alain Chapel for lunch at a restaurant run by one of the great masters of the period between 1950 and 1960. By one p.m., the chef was completely drunk, his legs dancing a kind of jig independent of the rest of his body and his speech hopelessly slurred. He said he was tired and needed to lie down, but assured us that he had prepared our meal in advance. And so it proved, though the *langoustines* were plastered with *sel de Guérande*, and the sea bass was invisible beneath a mantle of ketchup.

But Pierre is not much of a drinker. He loves wine, every nuance of it, but other alcohol he can do without. When pressed, he will admit a preference for white burgundy. I remember the evening at the King Sitric at Howth, in Ireland, when he first tasted the Chablis and the Sauvignons de Saint-Bris made by Olivier de Moor, which are now staples of

Le Balzac and Gaya. "Ça, c'est bon," he said, with a childlike glint in his eye and a conspiratorial grin. When he talks about wine Pierre is like the Ramonet family, especially the grandfather, Pierre Ramonet, who used to say, "Là, il y a du vin" when he was pleased with one of his own Chassagne-Montrachets.

There is no need to wax lyrical and verbose about wine; there are quite enough buffoons in the world to supply words. To my way of thinking, good wine deserves to be consumed without fuss. Silent approval is the best compliment, and that goes for many other pleasures as well. If you happen to be reading a page from Chateaubriand, Pasolini, Alfred Jarry, or George Orwell, you won't appreciate somebody starting up a jackhammer right outside your window. If you're in a great restaurant you'll want silence there too, for, as Cambacérès justly remarked, one should listen to what one eats.

J.–F. A.

2002

WHOLE SQUAB ROASTED WITH SWEET RED PEPPER,
GREEN PAPAYA AND ALMOND TUILES, ICED PEAR PULP WITH CORIANDER

Serves 4

ROAST SQUAB

4 FAT GAUTHIER SQUABS

3 TABLESPOONS PEANUT OIL

1/4 CUP UNSALTED BUTTER

PEEL OF 1 ORANGE

PEEL OF 1 LEMON

1 SPRIG THYME

1 GLASS RED WINE (SYRAH)

1 GLASS MINERAL WATER

1/2 TEASPOON GROUND BLACK PEPPER

1 TEASPOON VADOUVAN (SEE PAGE 196)

1/2 TEASPOON CORNSTARCH (OPTIONAL)

4 RED BELL PEPPERS

4 SLICES FOIE GRAS

2 TABLESPOONS OLIVE OIL

ALMOND TUILES

2/3 CUP ALL-PURPOSE FLOUR

1 1/2 TABLESPOONS SUGAR

1 TABLESPOON ALMOND FLOUR

1/2 CUP MELTED UNSALTED BUTTER

3 3/4 OUNCES EGG WHITES (ABOUT 3)

FLAKED ALMONDS

ROAST SQUAB

Sear the squabs quickly in a heavy-bottomed casserole with a little of the peanut oil and a pat of butter. Remove them when browned, but still raw. Remove the breasts and set them aside in the refrigerator. Crush the carcasses and thighs and brown them well in the casserole. Add the orange and lemon peels and the sprig of thyme, and moisten gradually with the wine, letting the juices reduce completely before each new addition of liquid. Finally, add the mineral water and cook for 40 minutes.

Remove the casserole from the heat, add the black pepper and the *vadouvan*, and leave to infuse for 5 minutes. Strain the juice and reduce to about 3 1/2 tablespoons (bind, if necessary, with a pinch of cornstarch). Whisk the sauce with 2 teaspoons butter, adding it bit by bit. Correct the seasoning, set aside, and keep warm.

Pass the bell peppers over an open flame to char their skins. Then remove the skins, open them through their tops, and remove the seeds.

Open up the squab breast (like a book), and slip a slice of seasoned foie gras between the flaps. Close the fillets on the foie gras, truss them up with kitchen string, and refrigerate for 15 minutes. Next, brown the squab breasts in a pat of melted butter, remove their skins and strings, and insert them into the peppers. Place the peppers in an ovenproof dish with some olive oil and a pat of butter and bake for 5–6 minutes in an oven preheated to 350°F. Keep warm for 20 minutes after cooking, so the squab stays tender and slightly pink.

ALMOND TUILES

Mix the all-purpose flour, sugar, and almond flour. Add the melted butter, then the egg whites. Fold together using a small spatula.

Spread the dough on a nonstick baking tray, sprinkle with flaked almonds, and bake for 6–8 minutes in an oven preheated to 325°F.

Remove the *tuiles* and leave them to cool on a rack. Set aside in a dry place.

BRUNOISE OF FRUIT

Slice the green papaya, the apple, and the half mango in $1/16$-inch cubes—the French call this a *brunoise*—tossing them into a bowl as you go. Moisten with the juice of a lime. Add the pulped garlic and the chopped parsley with salt. Set aside at room temperature.

ICED PEAR PULP

Dice the pears and sauté them in a nonstick pan. Deglaze with the lemon juice and pear eau-de-vie. Pour all this into a bowl, add the fresh cream and yogurt, and purée in a blender. Set aside for 1 hour in the freezer. Just before serving, add the chopped coriander to the iced pulp.

BEFORE SERVING

Spoon the *brunoise* into the centers of the plates and lay a *tuile* on top of each pile. Present your squab-stuffed peppers to your guests, then cut off the ends and slice the squab into two or three pieces with the pepper around it. As carefully as you can, lay the slices of squab and pepper on top of the *tuiles* in the plates. Serve the iced pear pulp separately in small cups.

BRUNOISE OF FRUIT

$3^1/2$ OUNCES GREEN PAPAYA

1 GREEN APPLE

$1/2$ MANGO

JUICE OF 1 LIME

$1/2$ GARLIC CLOVE, CRUSHED

2 SPRIGS FLAT-LEAF PARSLEY

ICED PEAR PULP

3 PEARS, PEELED

JUICE OF 1 LEMON

SPLASH OF PEAR EAU-DE-VIE

SCANT $1/2$ CUP HEAVY CREAM

1 POT PLAIN YOGURT

3 SPRIGS CORIANDER, LEAVES FINELY CHOPPED

SALT AND PEPPER

RED PEPPERS

THEY'RE VERY GOOD SALTED, BUT INCOMPARABLY DELICIOUS SWEETENED:

SWEET SUGAR PEPPERS—SUGAR-PRESERVED WITH SAFFRON—GO BEAUTIFULLY WITH

VANILLA ICE CREAM AND WILD STRAWBERRIES.

Gaya in the Rue du Bac

Rue du Bac is named after the boats (*bacs*) that used to ferry people and goods across the Seine at the point where it now meets the river at the Pont Royal. Pierre Gagnaire's Left Bank restaurant, Gaya, is three blocks from the bridge.

One interesting aspect of Gaya is that the diners there seem inclined to talk to people at neighboring tables (though always with sensitivity and courtesy). I believe this is because they are inordinately happy, as happy as children, to be sharing in a cuisine that is at once naïve, ingenious, funny, and subtle. *Jus de fraise au savagnin, gambas aux cacahuètes et ketchup Gaya, lichettes de jambon bellotta sur coeur de laitue et purée d'oseille*—if just one of these dishes doesn't make you feel altogether better and uncommonly sociable, then you really are a curmudgeon and a hypochondriac.

In Gagnaire's rue du Bac restaurant it is the cuttlefish ink *croque-monsieur* that is black, not the mood; indeed, the rue du Bac in general is one of the best streets in Paris for high spirits, which always engender a lusty appetite. The Galerie Maeght, for example, is nearby, a place where you are very likely to glimpse a cheerful gouache by Miró. I would also venture that your mind's eye will quickly establish a joyous connection between Gagnaire's grilled red peppers with sea snails, cockles, almonds, and infusion of prawns and a Tapiès painting of Catalonia that may chance to be in that same gallery's window.

The first time I had lunch at Gaya, the diner at the neighboring table was the head of Rivages, a Paris publishing house. Between carefully chosen comments on his authors, from Dennis Lehane to Elizabeth Taylor, he informed me that he owned vineyards in the Saumur appellation. I knew his wines—I'd tasted them at the Colette table at the Grand Vefour. It was probably high time I met a man like that, with whose books and wine I was already well acquainted. Since then I have always thought of Gaya as the perfect place for chance encounters.

And the first time I had dinner at Gaya, my neighbors were named Alain and Anne, and they too were delightful. They had come to sample Pierre's selected works on the Left Bank, before tackling his masterpieces on the Right—a refined approach that was in keeping with their conversation, which was delicate and serene. Our exchanges were erratic, given that good manners in such situations require frequent withdrawals into silence and the diminishing contents of one's plate. Alas, larger doses of Laurent-Perrier Ultra Brut than Alain and Anne were drinking are generally required to sustain conversation with people you don't know.

The menu at Gaya, with its *plats insolites* and *plats essentiels,* its *marée noble* and *marée modeste,* offers a perfect glimpse of where cooking has come from, and where it is heading. The everlasting nature of *sole meunière,* the novelty of mangos, grapefruit with wasabe, and *pétales de cabillaud*—they're all there. All other things being equal, at Gaya and along the rue du Bac you're bound to learn a lot and you're sure to be happy.

J.–F. A.

2002

"UNE ORIENTALE"

RED PEPPER JELLY WITH SAFFRON, BABY PATTYPAN SQUASH WITH PEACH AND TOMATO,
SQUAB PASTILLA, CREAM OF ALMONDS WITH SALTED HAZELNUTS,
BOUQUETIÈRE OF BABY CARROTS

Serves 6

RED PEPPER JELLY

4 SWEET RED BELL PEPPERS

1/3 CUP SUGAR

2 TABLESPOONS WATER

2 LEAVES OF GELATIN, SOFTENED IN COLD WATER

2–3 TEASPOONS SAFFRON THREADS

SCANT 1/2 CUP RED CURRANT JUICE

1/2 LEMON

SALT

BABY PATTYPAN SQUASH

6 BABY PATTYPAN SQUASH

1 SPRIG THYME

1 SPLASH OLIVE OIL

2 GARDEN-RAISED TOMATOES

2 WHITE PEACHES

2 TABLESPOONS OLIVE OIL

2 TABLESPOONS ARBUTUS FLOWER HONEY

1 SMALL FLAKE MACE

PINCH OF VADOUVAN (SEE PAGE 196)

SPLASH OF SHERRY VINEGAR

BOUQUETIÈRE OF CARROTS

12 SMALL CARROTS WITH THEIR TOPS

JUICE OF 1 LEMON

1 TEASPOON ARGAN OIL

1/2 TEASPOON GROUND CUMIN

PINCH OF SALT

RED PEPPER JELLY

The day before:

Broil the bell peppers in an oven preheated to 425°F. Remove skins and seeds. Purée the peppers in a blender, place them in a dampened kitchen towel, and press well. Save the resultant juice and refrigerate overnight (save the pulp for another use).

The next morning:

Make a syrup with the sugar and water, and add the pepper juice to make about 1²/₃ cups of liquid. Dissolve the softened gelatin in the hot liquid and add the saffron. Cover and leave to infuse for 30 minutes at room temperature. Sharpen this preparation with the red currant juice and a few drops of lemon juice, then salt lightly. Pour the mixture into small cups and set aside in the refrigerator.

BABY PATTYPAN SQUASH

Cut each squash in half, grill them in a nonstick pan, then roast for 5 minutes in an oven preheated to 375°F with a sprig of thyme and a splash of oil.

To remove the skins of the tomatoes and peaches, douse them quickly first in boiling water, and then in icy water. Peel and cut them in quarters.

Put the peeled and quartered peaches and tomatoes in a sauté pan and cook them with the olive oil, honey, mace, *vadouvan*, and a splash of vinegar over very low heat for 40 minutes.

BOUQUETIÈRE OF CARROTS

Peel the carrots and cut their tops to 1¹/₄ inches. Cook them for a few minutes in a pan of boiling salted water, then drain (they must remain crunchy). Moisten them with lemon juice and add the argan oil, cumin, and a pinch of salt.

154

SQUAB PASTILLA

Cut the pastry sheets into 4¹/₂-inch circles. Brush them with clarified butter and brown them for 5 minutes in an oven preheated to 350ºF. Set aside at room temperature.

Remove the breasts of the squabs and set them aside. Pound the carcass and thighs in a mortar, then fry in a pat of butter and some oil. Discard the cooking fats, add the chicken stock to the pan little by little, and reduce for 40 minutes or until you have a scant cup of highly concentrated squab juice.

Brown the seasoned squab breasts in a little clarified butter and some oil. Remove them while they are still pink. Remove the skin, and set aside to keep warm in a dish covered with aluminum foil.

CREAM OF ALMONDS

Blend the almond paste with ²/₃ cup of squab cooking juices and a dab of heavy cream, to obtain a fairly thick mixture.

BEFORE SERVING

Slice the squab breasts into very thin slices (*aiguillettes*), coat them with the reduced squab juice, and sprinkle with pepper. Pour a little almond cream into each of six bowls, then apportion the *aiguillettes* of squab and the salted hazelnuts. Cover each bowl with a crackly *brique* leaf.

Arrange the peach and tomato quarters in soup plates, then serve each with a helping of baby squash halves. Mix the carrots, pomegranate seeds, and golden raisins together and divide them among the six soup plates. Serve cups of pepper jelly separately.

SQUAB PASTILLA

3 SQUABS

4 SHEETS OF THIN ORIENTAL PASTRY (FEUILLES DE BRIQUE)

2 TEASPOONS CLARIFIED UNSALTED BUTTER

2 TEASPOONS UNSALTED BUTTER

2 TABLESPOONS OIL

2¹/₈ CUPS CHICKEN STOCK (SEE PAGE 190)

CREAM OF ALMONDS

1¹/₂ TABLESPOONS ALMOND PASTE (50 PERCENT)

SCANT ¹/₂ CUP HEAVY CREAM

2 TABLESPOONS SALTED HAZELNUTS

2 TABLESPOONS GOLDEN RAISINS, PLUMPED IN WATER

¹/₄ FRESH POMEGRANATE

SALT AND PEPPER

"UNE ORIENTALE"

THIS WAS THE FIRST DISH IN WHICH I SET OUT TO EXPRESS A SENSATION:

NAMELY, MY EXACT MEMORY OF A FEW DAYS SPENT IN MOROCCO.

I NEEDED TO RENEW THE MENU AT THE RESTAURANT, BUT THE AIR AROUND ME

SEEMED TO BE FULL OF THE AROMAS OF SPICES AND MECHOUIS,

AND MY INNER EYE WAS STILL DAZZLED BY BRIGHT COLORS.

THIS, FOR ME, WAS THE ORIENT.

"DODO" LOBSTER WITH HOT BROTH,
BLOOD ORANGE SHERBET, AND GOAT CHEESE WITH CORIANDER

Serves 2

LOBSTER BROTH

1 EUROPEAN LOBSTER (ABOUT 2 POUNDS)

3$\frac{1}{2}$ TABLESPOONS OLIVE OIL

2 WHITE ONIONS

1 SMALL CELERY STALK

1 FRESH TOMATO, PEELED AND SEEDED

1 BOUQUET GARNI (PARSLEY, THYME, AND BAY LEAF, TIED WITH A LEEK)

2$\frac{1}{8}$ CUPS WHITE WINE (MEURSAULT)

PINCH OF CURRY POWDER

PINCH OF GROUND CINNAMON

DOUBLE PINCH OF PAPRIKA

PINCH OF COLOMBO SPICES

SPLASH OF OLIVE OIL

PEEL OF 1 LEMON

10 GRAINS CUBEBE PEPPER (LONG PEPPER)

1 GELATIN LEAF, SOFTENED IN COLD WATER

"DODO" SAUCE

$\frac{1}{2}$ SWEET RED BELL PEPPER

1 TABLESPOON OLIVE OIL

DICED FRESH FRUIT (1 PEACH, $\frac{1}{2}$ BANANA, 1 APPLE, 1 PEAR)

$\frac{1}{2}$ TEASPOON CURRY POWDER

1 GARLIC CLOVE, CRUSHED

PEEL OF 1 ORANGE

PEEL OF 1 LEMON

2$\frac{1}{2}$ CUPS HEAVY CREAM (HALF UNWHIPPED, HALF WHIPPED)

10 FRESH MINT LEAVES

10 LEMON VERBENA LEAVES

10 FRESH GREEN PEPPERCORNS, PACKED IN BRINE

2 TEASPOONS UNSALTED BUTTER

LOBSTER BROTH

Cook the lobster and remove the flesh from tail and claws. Pound the carcasses and sauté them in very hot oil. Add the chopped onions and the diced celery. Incorporate the tomato and the bouquet garni, moisten with white wine, and cook for 35 minutes over low heat. Allow to cool, then strain (you should have about 2$\frac{1}{8}$ cups of broth).

Brown the spices (curry, cinnamon, paprika, and colombo) in the oil. Moisten with a scant cup of lobster broth. Add the lemon peel and the *cubebe* pepper and bring to a boil. Dissolve the softened gelatin in the hot broth. Leave for 10 minutes, then strain. Leave the broth to gel in two small cups.

"DODO" SAUCE

Cut the half bell pepper in a small dice and sauté in the oil. Add the diced fruit and the curry. Moisten with the rest of the lobster broth, then incorporate the garlic, citrus peel, and the unwhipped half of the cream. Cook for 20 minutes over low heat. Add the mint and lemon verbena and leave for 5 minutes to infuse, covered. Blend, then strain the sauce, without pressing it; reduce by half, and incorporate the whipped cream (the remaining half) to obtain an ivory-colored sauce. At the last minute, add the green peppercorns and the fresh butter, bit by bit.

Cut the lobster flesh into slices, arrange these in the bottom of a casserole dish, and coat them with sauce. Slowly raise their temperature in an oven preheated to 325°F for 5–6 minutes (any longer and the flesh will harden).

"DODO" LOBSTER

GOAT CHEESE DISCS

Blend the bread crumbs and the almond powder with the coriander and parsley leaves (this should come out a beautiful tender green).
Blend the fresh goat cheese with the honey and fashion the mixture into 1½-inch rounds. Roll these in the green bread crumbs.

BEFORE SERVING

Serve the lobster in its own casserole dish. Arrange the goat cheese rounds on the plates. At the last minute, lay a cylinder of blood orange sherbet on the cheese rounds. Serve the broth separately in small cups.

To make the broth absolutely clear, you must clarify it. This is a delicate maneuver, but the result is worth the effort. Whip 1 egg white with 1 chopped leek, a handful of chervil, and some parsley stems. Pour this into the warm broth and cook over low heat for 30 minutes without stirring. The egg white will coagulate, clearing the broth little by little.

THE INTEREST OF THIS RECIPE LIES IN THE SHEER QUANTITY OF SPICES IT REQUIRES, AND THE HARMONY BETWEEN THEM. THE DODO WAS A FLIGHTLESS BIRD THAT ONCE INHABITED THE ISLAND OF MAURITIUS. IT IS NOW EXTINCT, AS EVERYONE KNOWS.

GOAT CHEESE DISCS

3½ OUNCES FRESH GOAT CHEESE

4–5 TABLESPOONS FRESH BREAD CRUMBS

1½ TABLESPOONS ALMOND POWDER

3 CORIANDER STEMS

½ BUNCH FLAT-LEAF PARSLEY, LEAVES PICKED

1½ TEASPOONS HONEY

2 SCOOPS BLOOD ORANGE SHERBET

SALT AND PEPPER

CORIANDER FLOWERS

CORIANDER FLOWERS ARE WONDROUSLY BEAUTIFUL:

FRAGILE, GRACEFUL, WITH A LINGERING, SLIGHTLY HOT TASTE.

THEY ARE A LOVELY EXTENSION OF THE CORIANDER LEAF. I AM GRATEFUL TO MONSIEUR PIL,

OUR GARDENER, WHO PROVIDES A STEADY SUPPLY OF THEM TO THE RESTAURANT.

"AROUND THE POTATO"

ACID ALMOND MINESTRONE
EMULSIFIED RED CURRANT JUICE

▪

POMPADOUR POTATO GNOCCHI WITH SAFFRON
ARTICHOKE AND ORANGE BROTH, AGED GOUDA AND HAZELNUTS

▪

SEA-SCENTED CREAM OF DITA

▪

COMTESSE APPLE, SWEET CEVENNES ONION, AND GUERNICA PEPPER

▪

DESSERTS:
AGRIA CRISPS; CRÈME PARESSEUSE WITH VINTAGE VENEZUELAN RUM; VELOUTÉ OF INDIAN MANGO;
JELLIED INFUSION OF LEMON VERBENA; CHARLOTTE OF SICILIAN PISTACHIOS;
ICED ZABAGLIONE OF TONKA BEANS, VANILLA, AND GINGER; OPALINE DE VITELOTTE WITH FARMHOUSE CIDER

POMPADOUR POTATO GNOCCHI WITH SAFFRON,
ARTICHOKE AND ORANGE BROTH, AGED GOUDA AND HAZELNUTS

POTATO GNOCCHI

Cook the potatoes in their skins in a large pot of boiling salted water for about 40 minutes. Remove the skins while still hot and press the flesh through a *tamis* (a fine-mesh, drum sieve). Put 2¹/₂ ounces in a big bowl and incorporate the Parmesan cheese, flour, and egg yolk, mixing well between each addition. Season with salt and add the saffron. Work this preparation until the potato and flour paste is uniform in texture. Shape into a long sausage shape, ¹/₂ inch thick, on a board dusted with flour; then divide the dough into short lengths for the gnocchi, shaping them with your fingers.

Poach the gnocchi in 1 quart of salted water with the chicken stock added. Drain and place in a baking dish. Pour a little artichoke broth over them and dot with small pats of butter.

At the last moment, place the gnocchi in a hot oven (350°F) for 5 minutes.

HAZELNUTS

Roll the hazelnuts in the beaten egg white, sprinkle with salt, and dry in the oven (250°F) for 30 minutes.

ARTICHOKE BROTH

Separate the artichoke leaves from the hearts, then cut around the hearts with a very sharp knife and rub them with half a lemon. Place in a pot of cold water with a little lemon juice, flour, and oil and cook for 35 minutes. Drain the hearts, set aside the leaves, and cut the hearts into quarters.

Cook the artichoke leaves in the chicken stock with the orange peel for 25 minutes. Leave to infuse for a further 10 minutes, then strain the broth (it should be greenish and slightly bitter).

BEFORE SERVING

Lay a couple of spoonfuls of gnocchi on each plate, set a quarter of a warm artichoke heart beside them, and cover with a few shards of Gouda cheese. Sprinkle with the toasted hazelnuts and pour over some hot artichoke broth.

Serves 4

POTATO GNOCCHI

2 LARGE POTATOES

3 TABLESPOONS GRATED PARMESAN

¹/₄ CUP FLOUR PLUS ¹/₄ CUP TO WORK THE DOUGH

1 EGG YOLK

PINCH OF POWDERED SAFFRON

3¹/₂ TABLESPOONS CHICKEN STOCK (SEE PAGE 190)

4 TEASPOONS UNSALTED BUTTER

HAZELNUTS

12 FRESH SHELLED HAZELNUTS

1 EGG WHITE, BEATEN

ARTICHOKE BROTH

5 ARTICHOKES

¹/₂ LEMON

PINCH OF FLOUR

SPLASH OF PEANUT OIL

1²/₃ CUPS CHICKEN STOCK

PEEL OF 1 ORANGE

¹/₄ POUND AGED GOUDA CHEESE, SHAVED WITH A VEGETABLE PEELER

SALT AND PEPPER

POMPADOUR POTATO GNOCCHI

GOOD GNOCCHI ARE COMFORTING AND EASY TO MAKE—AN EXCELLENT DISH FOR THE NOVICE COOK.

THEY'RE FUN, AND THEY COME IN MANY COLORS: BLACK, RED, YELLOW, AND BLUE—MAGIC, REALLY.

SUPRÊME OF HEN PHEASANT
STUFFED WITH ALMOND AND PISTACHIO PASTE AND ROASTED IN COLOMBO, ENDIVE AND BROCCOLI FLOWER PANCAKES

Serves 4–6

HEN PHEASANT

2 HEN PHEASANTS

3¹/₂ TABLESPOONS UNSALTED BUTTER, SOFTENED

2¹/₂ TABLESPOONS ALMOND PASTE (50 PERCENT)

1¹/₂ TEASPOONS UNSWEETENED PISTACHIO PASTE

1 TABLESPOON CRUSHED TOASTED PISTACHIOS

1³/₄ OUNCES PIG'S CAUL

THYME FLOWERS

SPLASH OF OLIVE OIL

3 TABLESPOONS UNSALTED BUTTER

2 TEASPOONS CLARIFIED UNSALTED BUTTER (SEE PAGE 191)

2 SPRIGS THYME

¹/₂ BOTTLE CHAMPAGNE

1¹/₄ CUPS CHICKEN STOCK (SEE PAGE 190)

1 TEASPOON YELLOW COLOMBO CURRY POWDER

1 TABLESPOON WHIPPED CREAM

ENDIVE AND BROCCOLI PANCAKES

4 ENDIVES

1 TABLEPOON UNSALTED BUTTER

1³/₄ OUNCES GREEN WALNUTS, PREVIOUSLY MARINATED IN MILK

7 OUNCES BROCCOLI FLOWERS

HEN PHEASANT

Debone the pheasants and set aside the breasts (*suprêmes*). Crush the thighs and carcasses; set aside.

Mix together the softened butter, almond paste, and pistachio paste; add the crushed, toasted pistachios. Form into a sausage shape, wrap in plastic wrap, and place in the refrigerator.

Stuff the pheasant *suprêmes* by slipping a slice of almond and pistachio paste under the skin. Wrap all this in caul and truss with kitchen string. Marinate these stuffed *suprêmes* with the thyme flowers and oil for 2 hours.

Crush and cook thighs and carcasses in a little butter and oil until brown. Add the thyme sprigs. Moisten with a glass of champagne and reduce. Add more champagne and reduce once again. Leave to cool, then strain the *jus*. Set aside.

In a frying pan, sear the *suprêmes* in the clarified butter. Add fresh butter and cook for 10 minutes more over moderate heat, covered, basting the meat and turning it over regularly. Remove the *suprêmes* from the heat and set them aside in a dish, covered with aluminum foil.

Sprinkle colombo curry powder in the pan, cook the spice mixture for a minute in the cooking fat, deglaze with 1¹/₄ cups of pheasant *jus*, and reduce over low heat, incorporating 2 tablespoons of butter and the whipped cream little by little. Check the seasoning, and strain the sauce carefully.

ENDIVE AND BROCCOLI PANCAKES

Pull off the leaves of the endives and sauté them for a few minutes in a little butter. When they are more or less limp, shape them into small pancakes to enclose the green walnuts. Place them in a buttered dish with a tablespoon of the pheasant *jus*.

Shred the broccoli with a mandoline to remove the flowers. Plunge the flowers in a pot of boiling salted water for 2 minutes, and drain carefully on kitchen towels. Peel the broccoli stems (discarding the outside) and chop the core into 1¹/₄-inch lengths. Cook in the same way in boiling salted water and drain.

At the last moment, place the endive pancakes in an oven preheated to 350°F for a few minutes, then warm the broccoli core for a few minutes with a little sauce.

SUPRÊME OF HEN PHEASANT

THICKENED CREAM

Mix together (but don't whip) the milk, cream, and egg yolks with the pheasant *jus*. Pour this into small cups and cook for 25–30 minutes in a bain-marie in an oven preheated to 300°F.

BEFORE SERVING

Slice the pheasant *suprêmes* in two lengthwise and lay them on top of the warm broccoli cores. Lay an endive pancake on each mound of thickened cream, at room temperature, and sprinkle with broccoli flowers. Serve the colombo sauce separately.

THESE DAYS GAME IS ROUGHLY HANDLED, SCORNED, MOCKED, AND CRITICIZED AT EVERY TURN. WE COOKS MUST REMAIN INVENTIVE IF THE TRADITION OF GAME COOKING IS TO ENDURE. WE MUST GRAPPLE WITH A PRODUCT THAT IS OFTEN MUCH MORE CIVILIZED AND TAME THAN IT OUGHT TO BE. WE MUST MAGNIFY THE HEN PHEASANT BY EMPLOYING ONLY ITS BREAST; WE MUST USE THE THIGHS FOR THEIR JUICE ALONE AND DISMISS THE IDEA OF ROASTING ALTOGETHER, BECAUSE ROASTING INEVITABLY DRIES A PHEASANT OUT. IN THIS RECIPE, THE MEAT IS COOKED OVER LOW HEAT AND BASTED FREQUENTLY SO THAT IT PRESERVES ALL ITS CHARACTER.

THICKENED CREAM

1/4 CUP MILK

2/3 CUP HEAVY CREAM

2 EGG YOLKS

1 SCANT CUP PHEASANT JUS (PRODUCED DURING PREPARATION)

SALT AND PEPPER

SCALLOPS OF DUCK MARINATED IN PEAR BRANDY,
RED TUNA FILLET AND HAZELNUT CRUMBLE, DUCK SAUCE WITH BITTER CHOCOLATE,
POTATO GALETTE WITH FOIE GRAS

Serves 4

HAZELNUT CRUMBLE

3 TABLESPOONS UNSALTED BUTTER

2¹/₂ TABLESPOONS SUPERFINE SUGAR

¹/₄ CUP TOASTED HAZELNUTS

¹/₃ CUP BREAD CRUMBS

3 TABLESPOONS POTATO STARCH

2 TABLESPOONS FRESH HERBS (CHIVES, TARRAGON, CORIANDER, FLAT-LEAF PARSLEY)

DUCK AND RED TUNA

5–6 OUNCES RED TUNA FILLET

1 DUCK, DEBONED (CARCASS AND THIGHS, CRUSHED)

3¹/₂ TABLESPOONS EAU-DE-VIE POIRE WILLIAM (PEAR BRANDY)

2 TABLESPOONS OLIVE OIL

FRESHLY GROUND BLACK PEPPER

2 TABLESPOONS GOOSE FAT

2 TEASPOONS UNSALTED BUTTER

2¹/₈ CUPS CHICKEN STOCK (SEE PAGE 190)

2 SPRIGS THYME

¹/₂ BAY LEAF

HANDFUL OF PARSLEY STEMS

1 SLICE SMOKED BACON

¹/₂ OUNCE BITTER CHOCOLATE (PÂTE DE CACAO)

HAZELNUT CRUMBLE

The day before:

Blend all the ingredients together. Shape them into a sausage and wrap in plastic wrap. Set aside in the refrigerator overnight.

The next day:

Cut the crumble into slices, place them on a nonstick baking sheet, and bake for 5 minutes in an oven preheated to 425°F.

DUCK AND RED TUNA

Dice the tuna into 1¹/₂-inch cubes. Set aside in the refrigerator.

Marinate the duck breasts with the eau-de-vie, a little oil, and ground black pepper in a dish for 30 minutes. Cover with plastic wrap and place in the refrigerator.

Sear the duck breasts in a tablespoon of goose fat for 5 minutes, taking care that they remain rare. Leave them to cool in a small cast-iron dish with a pat of butter.

Brown the crushed duck thighs and carcass in a tablespoon of goose fat. When they are golden, discard the cooking fat, then gradually add the chicken stock. Add the sprigs of thyme, the bay leaf, and the parsley stems. Simmer for 1¹/₂ hours. Allow to cool and strain. Add the slice of smoked bacon and reduce to about 1 cup. Strain again to remove the bacon, let cool, and refrigerate.

Cut the duck breasts lengthwise into long strips (*aiguillettes*) and return them to the dish with their warm marinade.

POTATO GALETTE

Briefly sauté the foie gras scallops in a nonstick pan for 1 minute on each side. Set aside to cool.

Shape the peeled potatoes into large, cork-shaped pieces 3/4 of an inch in diameter. Cook the trimmings in water with a little salt, drain carefully, and press through a *tamis* (a fine-mesh, drum sieve). Season the purée with salt and pepper.

Cut the potatoes into very thin slices, using a mandoline, and mix them with the melted clarified butter. Arrange these slices on the bottoms and sides of small nonstick cake molds in a rosette pattern, allowing them to overlap the edges of the mold.

Place a little of the potato purée at the bottom of each mold, lay a slice of foie gras on top, cover with more mashed potato, and fold the projecting potato slices back over the top. Press down the galettes with your hand (this will make them more consistent and easier to turn out) and bake for 15 minutes in an oven preheated to 400°F.

BEFORE SERVING

Reheat the duck stock, bind it with the bitter chocolate, and check the seasoning.

Place the slices of hazelnut crumble on the plates, apportion the duck *aiguillettes* and the cubes of raw tuna.

Turn out the potato galettes on small side plates.

Serve the juice separately.

THIS IS A RISKY, WITTY DISH: VERY GAGNAIRE, IF I MAY SAY SO MYSELF.
IT IS A PERFECTLY SENSIBLE WAY OF MARRYING DUCK AND TUNA—BUT IT WAS
SOMETHING OF A DISASTER IN PRACTICE. NOT EVERYONE IN THE KITCHEN QUITE
UNDERSTOOD IT; THEY HAD A DIFFICULT TIME REGULATING THE SUBTLE RELATIONSHIPS
IN THE COOKING, SEASONING, CUTTING, AND VOLUME OF EACH INGREDIENT.
I'LL IRON OUT THE GLITCHES ONE OF THESE DAYS.

POTATO GALETTE

1 POUND AGRIA POTATOES

4 SCALLOPS DUCK FOIE GRAS (ABOUT 1 OUNCE EACH)

3 TABLESPOONS CLARIFIED UNSALTED BUTTER

SALT AND PEPPER

Time's Lessons

We think of time as ticking by like a metronome, yet there is nothing in nature more discontinuous, erratic, fragmented, and tattered than time. To begin with, there's the time beyond our ken, the time that passes when we're asleep or ill. Then there's the subjective time François Truffaut speaks of in *La peau douce*—a blinding flash of understanding that expands the thirty seconds the elevator takes to reach your floor, or on the contrary shrinks the moments to nothing. At moments like that, there is no doubt: The airplane you see climbing into the sky is taking away the woman you love.

In Pierre Gagnaire's youth he wore the chef's uniform like a full suit of armor, and was about as keen to continue in the profession as he was to become a taxi driver or a commercial traveler. The *brigades* of classic French kitchens suffocated him more than crowds in soccer stadiums; and as far as he was concerned, the immutable recipes in great cookery books by men like Escoffier offered an unspeakably dull future. He sincerely disagreed with Raymond Radiguet's sentiment that "our greatest pleasures are born of habit."

The Gagnaire family restaurant at Saint-Priest-en-Jarez had an excellent reputation in the region. The Gagnaires cooked their *jambon dans le foin* as if to demonstrate that nature is never far from the table. But Pierre began to take a real interest in cooking only at the time his father turned away from it. It was then that he started dreaming up dishes that rocked the boat of established tastes. His *pochette de saint-pierre aux poivrons doux* gave him his first chance, endowing him with an elegance that has accompanied him ever since.

For Pierre Gagnaire, as for any creative individual, time has proved an invaluable teacher. Every creator has to construct a rationale for himself; genius, as the musician Michel Devy used to say, "doesn't emerge from a pond with a lily pad on its head."

And Pierre himself likes to repeat that time helps people find new directions. "There's everything I'm learning from Hervé This, for example, about cooking methods, jellies, and juices. At the same time, the Saint-Étienne saga continues— a thread still connects me to those years. Now I'm old enough to have two sons who've chosen not to follow me into the *métier*, while for me the adventure is just the same as it was years ago when we were casting about for a title for my first book. *La cuisine immédiate*—that's the key. You have to pretend for a moment that you've forgotten all the recipes, norms, and requirements of the profession, in order to feel that you are improvising outside them. In the early days we liked free jazz, and cooking could still do with a bit more freedom."

Pierre has paid dearly for his liberty. But at the same time he has earned, somewhere between the poles of Saint-Étienne and Paris, a certain detachment that he lacked in the beginning of his career. "It seemed to me that I had to keep hold of the happy, playful aspect of Saint-Étienne by investing more of myself in my work. I wanted to make my brand of cuisine clearer and easier to read. Maybe I was a bit fed up with remarks like 'I had dinner at Gagnaire's last night. I haven't a clue what I ate, but it was fabulously good.' These days, clients ought to understand—without my having to tell them—that hot avocados really are delicious and that chorizos marry wonderfully well with Jerusalem artichokes.

"Intuition is all very well, but it's not a bad thing to actually test one's intuitions. In Paris I never stop tasting the food I concoct—I certainly didn't do that systematically when I was in Saint-Étienne."

Pierre's time is more fluid these days than it used to be. He has the kind of energy that enjoys seeing the hours go by at a snail's pace. And there is still no lily pad on his head, only a lock of hair that tumbles forward. He smoothes it back with both hands, a gesture recognized by everyone who goes to his restaurant regularly, whether they are former professional soccer players from Saint-Étienne or captains of industry.

It is Pierre Gagnaire's signature, and it is as unique to him as his cuisine.

J.–F. A.

GARLIC RAVIOLI WITH TRUFFLES,

SEMI-PRESERVED VEAL LIVER, MONSIEUR PIL'S SPRING VEGETABLES,
COCOTTE OF VEAL SWEETBREADS IN FRESH HAY, ROCKET JUICES WITH TARRAGON,
BORDEAUX CANNELÉS WITH BEEF MARROW AND VEAL KIDNEY,
CONDENSED GUINNESS AND GRAPEFRUIT SOUR ESSENCE WITH TURMERIC

Serves 4

GARLIC RAVIOLI

2¼ CUPS FLOUR

1 CUP EGG YOLKS (ABOUT 13)

3 PINCHES OF SALT

1 TABLESPOON OLIVE OIL

4 UNPEELED GARLIC CLOVES

3 SMALL POTATOES (NEW POTATOES OR RATTE FINGERLING POTATOES)

2 TABLESPOONS CHICKEN STOCK (SEE PAGE 190)

TRUFFLE SAUCE

⅓ CUP SUMMER TRUFFLES, SLICED

4 TEASPOONS UNSALTED BUTTER

SCANT ½ CUP RED PORT

1 SCANT CUP VEAL ESSENCE

VEAL LIVER

⅔ POUND CALF'S LIVER (1 THICK PIECE)

SALT

PINCH OF THYME

PINCH OF MARJORAM FLOWERS

3 TEASPOONS CLARIFIED UNSALTED BUTTER

GOOSE FAT

PEEL OF 1 ORANGE OR LEMON

5 WHOLE PEPPERCORNS

2 JUNIPER BERRIES

SPRING VEGETABLES

1 POUND BABY SPRING VEGETABLES: CARROTS WITH THEIR TOPS, BABY TURNIPS, WHITE ONIONS WITH THEIR TOPS, BABY SQUASH AND ZUCCHINI, FRENCH GREEN BEANS, CABBAGE

GARLIC RAVIOLI

Prepare the pasta dough: Knead the flour with the egg yolks, salt, and oil. Do not add water—the dough needs to be very firm and stiff. Wrap in plastic wrap and set aside for 2 hours before rolling out the dough very thinly. Cut the garlic cloves in half without peeling them, place them in a nonstick baking pan cut sides down, and pour on a little oil. When they are lightly colored, place them on a sheet of aluminum foil and fold it over to form a papillote. Roast for 40 minutes in an oven preheated to 350°F. Unwrap the cooked garlic cloves, squeeze, and push the pulp through a *tamis* (a fine-mesh, drum sieve).

Boil the potatoes in water, peel them, and pass through a *tamis*. Gradually incorporate the potato purée with the garlic purée. Season, mold into little dome shapes, and place in the freezer to harden.

Lay a sheet of pasta dough on a floured working surface, place the domes of garlic and potato purée at intervals on it, and moisten the edges of the dough with a little water. Cover with a second sheet of pasta. Push the two layers of dough together with your fingers around the domes of purée. Cut each one out with a round pastry cutter.

Set aside the ravioli in the refrigerator on floured wax paper.

At the last moment, poach the ravioli for 5–6 minutes in chicken stock.

TRUFFLE SAUCE

Sweat the slices of summer truffle in butter, add the port, and reduce by three-quarters over low heat. Add the veal essence. Bring the sauce to a boil, pour it in a blender immediately and blend until smooth. Correct the seasoning and set aside.

VEAL LIVER

Season the liver with salt, thyme, and marjoram flowers. Sear quickly with a pat of clarified butter, place in a casserole with plenty of goose fat (the fat should partially cover the liver). Add the citrus peel, peppercorns, and juniper berries, cover, and poach in the fat for 1½ hours over very low heat. Allow to cool, and then drain. Slice the calf's liver in thin strips.

SPRING VEGETABLES

Clean the vegetables, leaving 1½ inches of tops attached in the case of the turnips and carrots. Cook individually and briefly in a saucepan of boiling salted water. Refresh in a bowl of ice water and drain.

VEAL KIDNEY

Heat a little oil with 1 ounce of diced kidney fat. Place the seasoned kidney in this mixture and cook for

2005

20 minutes. Pierce with the tip of a knife and set aside on a dish covered with foil to allow the blood to run out. Set aside. At the last minute, slice the kidney very thin.

VEAL SWEETBREADS

Sear the sweetbreads in a little clarified butter. Place in a small *cocotte* (casserole or casserole dish) with a little fresh butter and salt. Cook for 15–20 minutes on low heat, adding a little water from time to time to prevent the butter from burning and basting frequently.
Remove the sweetbreads, place the hay in the *cocotte,* and replace the sweetbreads on top of it. Add 2 tablespoons of manzanilla sherry, cover, and continue to cook for a few minutes over low heat. Set aside and keep warm.

ROCKET JUICE

Blend the rocket with the tarragon leaves and a glass of water. Squeeze the liquid from this mixture through a clean kitchen towel. Pour the green juice into a small saucepan, allow to coagulate for a moment over high heat, then strain the juice, retaining the coagulated green matter separately. Mix this with a little oil and a tablespoon of water. Reserve the rocket juice in a glass in the refrigerator.

BORDEAUX CANNELÉS

Whisk together the egg and egg yolk and incorporate the powdered sugar, rum, flour, and melted butter. Add the strained milk. Blend and pour the mixture into buttered cookie molds with fluted sides. Bake for 45 minutes in an oven preheated to 350°F, then turn out the *cannelés* onto a rack.
Poach the rounds of beef marrow briefly in a pot of boiling salted water. Drain, allow to cool, and then place on the warm *cannelés* in a small dish.

SOUR ESSENCE

Reduce, separately, the grapefruit juice and the Guinness until you have $3^1/_2$ tablespoons of each. Mix with the turmeric, reduce for 1 minute, strain, and set aside.

BEFORE SERVING

Place the ravioli in a timbale in front of the guests, with the vegetables in a casserole, the rocket juice in a sauceboat, and the *cannelés* in a pretty dish of their own.
Place the kidney slices in soup plates and coat with the sour essence. Cut the veal sweetbreads in four pieces, replace them in their casserole dish, and serve from there.

VEAL KIDNEY

1 KIDNEY PREPARED IN ITS OWN FAT (FIRM AND WHITE)

1 TABLESPOON OIL

VEAL SWEETBREADS

1 SET OF VEAL SWEETBREADS

4 TEASPOONS UNSALTED BUTTER

2 HANDFULS OF HAY

ROCKET JUICE

$^1/_2$ POUND ROCKET SALAD

$^1/_2$ BUNCH TARRAGON (LEAVES REMOVED FROM STEMS)

1 TABLESPOON OLIVE OIL

BORDEAUX CANNELÉS

I SCANT CUP MILK, WARMED AND INFUSED WITH HALF A VANILLA BEAN

1 EGG YOLK

1 EGG

2 TABLESPOONS MELTED AND COOLED UNSALTED BUTTER

1 SCANT CUP POWDERED SUGAR

$4^1/_2$ TABLESPOONS RUM

$^1/_3$ CUP PLUS 1 TABLESPOON FLOUR

4 ROUNDS OF PERFECTLY WHITE BONE MARROW

SOUR ESSENCE

$1^1/_4$ CUPS GRAPEFRUIT JUICE

$1^1/_3$ CUPS GUINNESS

$^1/_2$ TEASPOON GROUND TURMERIC

SALT AND PEPPER

GARLIC

EVERYONE LOVES IT, NOBODY WANTS IT: SO GARLIC MUST BE USED VERY SPARINGLY,

WITH ABSOLUTE FINESSE, SUBLIMATED AS IT IS IN ASIAN COOKING.

"LE NOIR"

BLACK CREAMED RICE WITH BLACK SARAWAK PEPPER, BLACK RADISH WITH
QUETSCH PLUMS, BRAISED VEAL SWEETBREADS WITH BLACK NYONS OLIVES AND
HORN-OF-PLENTY MUSHROOMS, TURNIP JELLY À LA DEMI-DEUIL,
OLIVE AND CUTTLEFISH MERINGUES

Serves 4

CREAMED RICE

5¼ OUNCES VÉNÉRÉ BLACK RICE

2 SMALL WHITE ONIONS

1 TABLESPOON UNSALTED BUTTER

1⅔ CUPS CHICKEN STOCK (SEE PAGE 190)

SALT

RADISH WITH PLUMS

1 TABLESPOON OLIVE OIL

1 BLACK RADISH

1 TABLESPOON CLARIFIED
UNSALTED BUTTER

3½ TABLESPOONS PORT

1 SCANT CUP CHICKEN STOCK

1⅛ POUNDS QUETSCHES, WITH
THEIR STONES

TURNIP JELLY

WHITE JELLY:

8 OUNCES PURÉED TURNIPS

1¼ CUPS HEAVY CREAM

⅛ OUNCE GELATIN, SOFTENED IN
COLD WATER

BLACK JELLY:

8 OUNCES PURÉED TURNIPS

1¼ CUPS CHICKEN STOCK

¼ CUP CUTTLEFISH INK

⅛ OUNCE GELATIN, SOFTENED IN
COLD WATER

CREAMED RICE

Sweat the finely chopped onion in a pat of butter, add the rice, and stir it well so that every grain is well coated. Pour in the chicken stock (twice the volume of the rice). Add salt, cover, and cook for 25 minutes in an oven preheated to 350°F. Remove 2 spoonfuls of the cooked but still firm-textured rice and put aside for the final stages. Place the rest of the black rice into a blender and purée with a little stock to create a creamy texture. Push this preparation through a *tamis* (a fine-mesh, drum sieve) and adjust the salt if needed.

At the last minute, put the creamed black rice through the blender again until velvety, then add the Sarawak pepper and the reserved cooked rice. Set aside.

RADISH WITH PLUMS

Slice the radish into 3¼-inch pieces and blanch them in a pot of boiling salted water. Drain and sauté in clarified butter. Moisten with the port and some chicken stock, cover, and cook for 30 minutes over low heat. Sauté the plums in the oil, again over low heat, cooking for about 15 minutes. Let cool at room temperature. Arrange the cooked plums on top of the braised radish slices.

TURNIP JELLY

The day before:

Prepare a white jelly: Bring the turnip purée to the boil with the heavy cream, then add the softened gelatin. Place the purée on a baking sheet lined with plastic wrap in a layer about ¼ inch deep. Leave to set in the refrigerator overnight.

Prepare a black jelly: Heat the turnip purée with the chicken stock, then add the cuttlefish ink and the softened gelatin. Place the purée on another baking sheet lined with plastic wrap, also in a layer about ¼ inch deep. Leave to set in the refrigerator overnight.

The next day:

Cut out rounds of jelly with a 2-inch cookie cutter, then cut these into quarters. Reassemble eight rounds, assembling two quarters of white jelly with two quarters of black jelly. Superimpose them in twos, to form a checkerboard pattern. Set aside in the refrigerator.

OLIVE AND CUTTLEFISH MERINGUES

Blanch the olives three times in boiling water. Drain well and then pit and chop them.

Whisk the egg whites until stiff, add some of the superfine sugar with the powdered egg white and the cuttlefish ink, and add the remaining sugar. Fold in the powdered sugar delicately with a spatula, followed by the lemon juice and chopped olives.

Pipe small sticks (*bâtonnets*) of this meringue mixture on a sheet of parchment paper and bake for 3 hours in an oven preheated to 300°F. Leave to cool, then store in an airtight box in a dry place.

BRAISED SWEETBREADS

Plunge the white cabbage leaves in a large saucepan of boiling water for 3 minutes, drain, and refresh under cold running water. Slice them in half.

Plunge the olives in a pan of boiling water and blanch for 3 minutes. Drain, pit, and chop coarsely.

Cook the mushrooms in a spoonful of water with a pat of fresh butter and a pinch of salt. Drain, chop coarsely, and mix with the olives and cabbage leaves.

Heat a little unsalted butter in a sauté pan, and add the sweetbreads. Season with salt and brown on all sides for about 20 minutes, basting often with the butter. When they are thoroughly caramelized and nearly cooked through, set them aside on a dish and cover with aluminum foil.

Pour a little veal essence into the pan and scrape up the brown bits on the bottom of the pan using a wooden spoon. Add the white cabbage, mushrooms, and chopped olives. Simmer for 6–7 minutes, stirring to blend the various scents and tastes.

Return the sweetbreads to the pan, sprinkle with black Sarawak pepper, and cover with a lid. Set aside and keep warm.

BEFORE SERVING

Pour the creamed black rice onto large plates.

Slide the checkerboard jellies onto small plates and pour the radish juice around them.

Arrange the black radish and plum mixture onto small plates, with a *vent des sables* meringue on each one.

Present the sweetbreads in their casserole dish, then delicately lower them, with their garnish, onto the black rice.

OLIVE AND CUTTLEFISH MERINGUES

1 OUNCE BLACK NYONS OLIVES

4 1/2 OUNCES EGG WHITES (ABOUT 4)

1/3 CUP SUPERFINE SUGAR

1 OUNCE POWDERED EGG WHITE

1–2 TEASPOONS CUTTLEFISH INK

1/2 CUP POWDERED SUGAR

1 TABLESPOON LEMON JUICE

BRAISED SWEETBREADS

4 WHITE CABBAGE LEAVES

2 TABLESPOONS BLACK NYONS OLIVES

9 OUNCES HORN-OF-PLENTY MUSHROOMS (CANTERELLUS CORNUCOPIODES)

1 1/2 TABLESPOONS UNSALTED BUTTER

4 SMALL SETS OF WHITE VEAL SWEETBREADS (3 1/2 OUNCES EACH)

1 SCANT CUP VEAL ESSENCE

SALT AND FRESHLY GROUND BLACK SARAWAK PEPPER

"LE NOIR"

LE NOIR—THIS DISH WAS INSPIRED BY BLACK RICE, RIZ VÉNÉRÉ. THIS IS A REMARKABLE GRAIN,

THE SMOOTHNESS AND SAVOR OF WHICH ARE SIMPLY ASTOUNDING. IT'S WONDERFUL WHEN ONE COMES

ACROSS DIFFERENT QUALITIES IN A FOOD, EACH WITH THE POTENTIAL TO YIELD A DIFFERENT TEXTURE.

GAMBAS DE PALAMÓS

MY CHILDHOOD EXPERIENCE OF SPAIN WAS OF A SPECIAL LIGHT AND A DEEP, ANGRY SEA—MOST UNUSUAL

FOR THE MEDITERRANEAN. THESE DELICIOUS GAMBAS, WHICH I DISCOVERED LONG AFTER IN

PALAMÓS, CATALONIA, REAWAKENED THE MEMORY OF ALL THAT.

PALAMÓS SHRIMP MACERATED IN AMONTILLADO SHERRY,
STUFFED WITH NIORA PEPPER AND PEANUT PASTE

Serves 4

SHRIMP AND NIORA PEPPER PASTE

8 PALAMÓS SHRIMP

3¹/₂ TABLESPOONS AMONTILLADO SHERRY

2 TABLESPOONS OLIVE OIL

1 GARLIC CLOVE, CRUSHED

PINCH OF CAYENNE PEPPER

10 WHOLE CORIANDER SEEDS

LARGE HANDFUL OF CHERVIL, CHOPPED

¹/₂ TEASPOON CARAWAY SEEDS

3¹/₂ TABLESPOONS WHITE WINE
(CHARDONNAY)

1 GLASS SPRING WATER

2 TABLESPOONS NIORA PEPPER PASTE (SEE
PAGE 195)

¹/₄ CUP CRUSHED, ROASTED PEANUTS

CORIANDER FLOWERS

JULIENNE AND BRUNOISE

1 CELERY STALK

3¹/₂ OUNCES CUCUMBER, PEELED AND
SEEDED

3¹/₂ OUNCES MANGO, PEELED AND SEEDED

THIN SLICES OF BREAD

SHRIMP AND NIORA PEPPER PASTE

Peel the shrimp, except for the last two rings of the shell (reserve the heads). Open the shrimp through the backs and remove the vein (the intestine). Pour the sherry into a deep dish that is narrow enough so that the shrimp will be just about submerged. Place the shrimp in the sherry and leave them to marinate for 30 minutes, basting from time to time.

Crush the heads to a pulp. Sauté them in olive oil with the garlic, pepper, coriander seeds, chervil, and caraway seeds.

Deglaze with the wine and spring water. Simmer for 15 minutes on low heat. Set aside to cool, then strain, pressing as hard as you can to obtain a syrupy juice. Reserve.

Mix a tablespoon of shrimp juice in with the Niora pepper paste. Add the roasted peanuts.

Stuff the shrimp with a little of this preparation. Take care not to put in too much, in order to preserve a balance among the ingredients.

JULIENNE AND BRUNOISE

Chop the celery stalk into very thin lengthwise pieces (julienne). Set aside. Cut the cucumber and mango into a small dice ¹/₁₆ inch square (*brunoise*).

Mix the sherry marinade with the rest of the shrimp juice. Add the *brunoise* of cucumber and mango.

BEFORE SERVING

Arrange the shrimp on very cold plates, along with some coriander flowers and the julienne of raw celery. Pour the juice into four cups. Serve with very thin slices of bread that have been dried out in the oven.

Haddock and the Common Man

I in his book *Et si c'était bon?*, Jean-Marcel Bouguereau, an admirer of Pierre Gagnaire, wrote: "A good cook gives precedence to his materials, like a chauffeur opening a car door for his master."

If the materials in question include Norwegian lobster, line-caught turbot, or pilgrim's scallops from Erquy, of course no "good cook" worth his salt would dream of treating them like Pierrot le Fou. Let there be nothing but noble ingredients, then, and let them be cooked by the eternal commoners of the kitchen. The doors of the big limousines shall continue to open for the rich and famous with their rumbling bellies, while the chefs go home on their bikes with a few potatoes in a box on the back. One doesn't like to mention class distinctions, but all the same . . .

For some years now Pierre Gagnaire has deliberately included in his menus certain uncouth fishes, along with sauces one would otherwise expect to find in a lower-end brasserie. What's a *lisette*, I ask you? A sort of mackerel? How about a maître d'hotel in a tracksuit while you're at it, or a sommelier with a badge saying "sommelier" on his lapel? Altogether bad form, in my opinion.

And as for haddock, it's only good for fish and chips. Maybe the experience of Sketch in London has turned Gagnaire into a Monty Python type, and this is just a bad joke. What could we want with a food that's suitable only for stevedores and market porters; why do we need this miserably smoked fish, in our resolutely non-smoking world?

When we last heard, the cook in the rue Balzac was trying to turn *sauce à l'échalotte* into something edible. We hope he's enjoying himself. *Lisettes*, haddock, *sauce à l'échalotte*—why not rubber tires?

Well, as it happens, Pierre Gagnaire's recipe for haddock with *amandes de mer*—wherein these humble shellfish have never been so perfectly themselves before, never so exquisitely sea-tasting—is like the aroma of a great chardonnay, simple but sumptuous. Joke over. The cook in the rue Balzac has a thousand times justified his interest in the *lisette* and the *sauce à l'échalotte*. We may find in this, among other merits, the ever more convincing evidence of his freedom.

J.-F. A.

MACKEREL

I PREFER TO CALL MACKEREL *LISETTES,* THE OLD FRENCH WORD FOR THEM. IT HAS A LIGHTER, MORE CHEERFUL RING

TO IT THAN *MAQUEREAUX.* THE MACKEREL IS A SIMPLE FISH THAT MANY PEOPLE DISMISS AS SECOND RATE.

ACTUALLY IT IS FULL OF CHARACTER, PROVIDED YOU HANDLE IT WITH INTELLIGENCE AND SENSITIVITY.

SPRING MENU — 2006

BEEF CONSOMMÉ: YOUNG RABBIT RILLETTES WITH COMBAVA LEAVES
RED TUNA FILLETS, EGGPLANT, MUSCATEL GRAPES, AND NIORA PEPPER PASTE

■

MEDALLION OF LOBSTER WITH CORIANDER
POLENTA WITH HORN-OF-PLENTY MUSHROOMS, CITRUS, AND MANGE-TOUT CHILI, CLEAR BROTH

■

NETTLE VELOUTÉ THICKENED WITH LETTUCE
LARGE OYSTERS (SPÉCIALES) WITH SHALLOT DRESSING, SMALL RYE QUENELLES AND BITTER SORBET WITH SAKE

■

RINGS OF HADDOCK AU NATUREL
ARTICHOKES STEWED WITH CELERY ROOT, SEARED FOIE GRAS,
BROCCOLI TIPS AND BABY LEEKS

■

POACHED SEA BREAM WITH MELTED BUTTER AND BERRIES
COLD TRIPE, LAUTREC GARLIC, AND GINGER, GRATIN OF BABY MASA ONIONS

■

SPRING CABBAGE SOUP WITH BLACK CRÈME CHANTILLY
FROG LEGS POULETTE

■

MILK-FED VEAL:
FILLET À L'ESTRAGON;
END CHOPS WITH MACE;
VEAL JUICE WITH VÉNÉRÉ BLACK RICE
RICOTTA WITH GREEN MANGO; TAMARIND JUICE AND GREEN CRESS LEAVES

■

SHEEP CHEESE:
PORTUGUESE SHEEP CHEESE IN A CRUSTY BRIOCHE;
CHEESE VELOUTÉ; OSSAU-IRATY CHEESE NUGGETS

■

PIERRE GAGNAIRE'S DESSERTS

RINGS OF HADDOCK AU NATUREL

Slice the haddock into very thin strips and arrange them in four rings (each 6 inches in diameter) on oiled parchment paper. Brush them with oil, sprinkle on a few drops of water and lemon juice, then place in an oven preheated to 425°F for 30 seconds. Slip the haddock rings immediately onto hot plates.

Accompany this dish with crème fraîche flavored with horseradish and slices of *pain grillé* (toast).

AND SO I HAVE COME FULL CIRCLE. ONE OF THE VERY FIRST RECIPES
RECORDED HERE—AN EXTREMELY SIMPLE ONE—IS FOR A POTATO GRATIN
'SEEN' MORE THAN LEARNED WITH MONSIEUR PAUL BOCUSE IN 1965.
THE LAST RECIPE, JUST AS SIMPLE AND CANDID,
IS A SUGGESTION FOR HADDOCK THAT I INVENTED WITH
FRIENDS AND FELLOW COOKS IN MIND.

Serves 4

1 HADDOCK FILLET, FINEST QUALITY OBTAINABLE

1 TEASPOON OLIVE OIL

SPRING WATER

1 LEMON

3^1/$_2$ TABLESPOONS CRÈME FRAÎCHE

HORSERADISH

PAIN GRILLÉ

BASIC RECIPES

BASIC RECIPES

BEEF CONSOMMÉ

3¹/₂ POUNDS SHORT RIBS OF BEEF

1¹/₂ TABLESPOONS COARSE SEA SALT

1 WHOLE CLOVE

1 BOUQUET GARNI (PARSLEY, THYME, AND BAY LEAF, TIED WITH A LEEK)

1 MEDIUM CARROT

1 CELERY STALK

1 ONION (L'OIGNON BRULÉ), CUT IN HALF AND BLACKENED IN A PAN ON THE CUT SIDE

1 SMALL LEEK

2 QUARTS SPRING WATER

FRESHLY GROUND BLACK PEPPER

The day before:

Place the meat, sea salt, clove, bouquet garni, and vegetables in a large pot, add the water, bring to a boil, and skim. Add the pepper and simmer until the meat is completely cooked, about 1¹/₂ hours.

Remove the meat from the pot with care. Leave the stock to cool for 15 minutes, then strain. Leave in the refrigerator overnight.

The next day:

Degrease the stock, completely removing the layer of fat that will have formed on the surface. Pour slowly into another saucepan, leaving the dregs behind. Bring the stock to a boil, strain through a fine-mesh sieve, and pour into small airtight containers and freeze. With beef consommé, the key is to let it rest. This allows the liquid to clarify without your having to resort to other, more complex measures (with egg whites) that are hard to carry off and take the edge off the taste.

CHICKEN STOCK

1 HEN (ABOUT 3¹/₂ POUNDS)

2¹/₂ POUNDS CHICKEN WINGS

2 CARROTS

2 ONIONS (L'OIGNON BRULÉ), CUT IN HALF AND BLACKENED IN A PAN ON THE CUT SIDE

2 BOUQUETS GARNIS (PARSLEY, THYME, BAY LEAF, AND CELERY, TIED WITH A LEEK)

1 ONION

Pound the chicken wings to a pulp. Place them in a pot and add enough water to cover. Add 1 carrot, the burnt onions, and 1 bouquet garni. Bring to a boil. When the liquid is bubbling, lower the heat, skim thoroughly, and cook for 1 hour on low heat. Strain the stock and leave to cool.

Place the hen in a cooking pot, pour the cold stock over it, and add enough water to cover the bird. Add the remaining carrot, the remaining bouquet garni, and the onion. Bring to a boil, skim. and cook for 2 hours over low heat. Set aside to cool, then strain through a fine sieve. Discard the hen.

Chill the stock in the refrigerator. When it is cold, degrease carefully and use immediately or pour into small containers for freezing.

CLARIFIED BUTTER

1/2 POUND (2 STICKS) UNSALTED BUTTER

Cut the butter into large cubes, place in a glass bowl, and melt slowly in a bain-marie. The butter will separate, with the fat rising to the surface and the milk solids sinking to the bottom. Skim off any foam that rises to the surface and pour off the clear butter. Use immediately or refrigerate for later use.

VEAL ESSENCE

2 1/4 POUNDS CALF'S BREAST, CHOPPED IN LARGE PIECES

3 1/2 TABLESPOONS OIL

1 CARROT

2 ONIONS

Brown the pieces of veal well in the oil in a heavy cast-iron casserole or Dutch oven. When the meat is golden, add the roughly chopped vegetables and leave to caramelize. Place the casserole in an oven preheated to 425°F for 10–15 minutes, stirring regularly. Put the casserole back on the stovetop and moisten the meat with water, scraping up the brown bits from the bottom of the casserole with a wooden spoon. Let the water evaporate entirely, then add 2 quarts of water and simmer for 90 minutes over very low heat.

Strain the stock, removing the meat and vegetables, then reduce by 50 percent over low heat, skimming from time to time.

Strain the veal essence (stock) very carefully through a sieve and place it in the refrigerator. When it is cold, remove the layer of congealed fat from the surface. Use immediately or pour the veal essence into small airtight containers for freezing.

Depending on its use, the essence can be bound with a little potato starch or a leaf of gelatin if you plan to serve it cold.

I LIKE TO GET THE SPECIFIC TASTE OF THE FOOD IN ANY MEAT ESSENCE. YOU SHOULDN'T OVERLOAD THE RECIPE WITH TOO MANY VEGETABLES OR HERBS. SLOW, GENTLE COOKING ALLOWS THE MEAT TO YIELD THE MAXIMUM SAVOR AND NATURAL GELATIN.

BASIC RECIPES

VEGETABLE STOCK

1 LEEK, WHITE PART ONLY

1 CARROT

1 CELERY STALK

1 FENNEL STALK

5¹/2 OUNCES (ABOUT 6 MEDIUM) MUSHROOMS

HANDFUL OF FLAT-LEAF PARSLEY STEMS

2 SPRIGS THYME

1 BAY LEAF

6¹/2 CUPS MINERAL WATER

PINCH OF COARSE SEA SALT

3 RIPE TOMATOES, SEEDED AND QUARTERED

HANDFUL OF FRESH HERBS (CHIVES, CHERVIL, AND LEMON BALM)

Dice all the vegetables (except the tomatoes) in similar sizes, and place them in a casserole with the aromatic herbs. Pour in the mineral water and the salt. Bring to a boil and cook very gently for 25 minutes. Clarify the stock by adding the quartered tomatoes and the fresh herbs at the last moment.

Take the casserole off the heat, cover, and leave to cool (the vegetables and herbs must remain in the stock to infuse).

Strain the stock very gently through a fine-mesh sieve. Use immediately or pour it into small airtight containers for freezing.

ROYALE DE POULE

2 QUARTS CHICKEN STOCK (SEE PAGE 190)

¹/2 CUP HEAVY CREAM

2¹/8 CUPS MILK

2 EGG YOLKS

SALT AND PEPPER

Mix all the ingredients. Strain the preparation through a fine-mesh sieve and let settle until the scum disappears.

Pour the *royale* into soup plates or bowls. Cover with plastic wrap to steam. The *royale* should be barely set and still trembling.

WHITE FISH CONCENTRATE (FUMET)

1 POUND WHITE SEA FISH BONES (SOLE, TURBOT, JOHN DORY, BRILL)

1 LEEK, WHITE PART ONLY, CHOPPED

2 SHALLOTS, FINELY CHOPPED

1 TABLESPOON UNSALTED BUTTER

2–3 MEDIUM WHITE MUSHROOMS, CHOPPED

1 BOUQUET GARNI (PARSLEY, BAY LEAF, AND THYME, TIED WITH A LEEK)

$3^1/_2$ TABLESPOONS DRY WHITE WINE

Rinse the fish bones carefully under cold running water. Set them aside for 1 hour in the refrigerator in a large bowl of water to purge them.

Soften the chopped leek and shallots in hot butter in a heavy-bottomed casserole. Add the drained fish bones, chopped mushrooms, bouquet garni, and white wine, and cook for 3–4 minutes. Add enough water to cover the bones and simmer very gently for a further 18 minutes, skimming carefully all the time.

When the cooking is done, take the casserole off the heat and leave the concentrate to settle for 20 minutes so that all its perfumes have time to meld. Strain the concentrate very gently to avoid clouding. Use immediately or pour into small airtight containers and freeze.

BEURRE DOUX

$3^1/_2$ TABLESPOONS SPRING WATER

PINCH OF SALT

A FEW DROPS OF LEMON JUICE

$^1/_2$ POUND (2 STICKS) VERY COLD UNSALTED BUTTER, CUT IN SMALL CUBES

Add salt and lemon to the water, bring it to a boil, and whisk the butter cubes into it. Allow to boil for 1 minute, so it will emulsify properly.

THIS RELATIVELY NEUTRAL BEURRE DOUX CAN BE USED TO SEASON VEGETABLES AND TO BRIGHTEN UP SHELLFISH OR A MOUSSELINE OF FISH. IT IS PERFECT FOR ROUNDING OUT TASTES. IN THE KITCHEN WE CALL IT 'LE CONFORTABLE.'

BASIC RECIPES

COOKING CRUSTACEANS

SALTED WATER (1–1¹/₂ TABLESPOONS COARSE SEA SALT PER QUART OF WATER)

Plunge the lobster or other crustacean into the boiling water. The cooking time depends on its size. For example, a 1¹/₂-pound lobster would be cooked in two stages: 3 minutes for the tail, from the moment the water hits the boil again; 2 minutes more for the claws.

In the case of crabs and spider crabs, allow 15–20 minutes.

Whatever the crustacean, it is important to leave it to cool for a while in the cooking water before you drain it.

CHANTILLY FOIE GRAS IN THE STYLE OF HERVÉ THIS

¹/₂ POUND RAW FRESH FOIE GRAS

¹/₄ CUP CHICKEN STOCK (SEE PAGE 190)

¹/₄ CUP RED PORT

1 GELATIN LEAF (¹/₈ OUNCE), SOFTENED IN COLD WATER

SALT AND PEPPER

Squeeze the foie gras through a sieve and set it aside.

Heat the chicken stock with the port and softened gelatin. Pour this preparation—it shouldn't be very hot—over the foie gras. Process all this in the blender until creamy, and correct the seasoning. Pour the mixture into a bowl set in crushed ice and whip it like *crème chantilly* (whipped cream). If the "chantilly" separates, melt it over low heat, and repeat the entire operation.

The chantilly foie gras can be more or less firm, depending on the use you have for it.

JODHPUR MIXTURE

1 TEASPOON POWDERED ORANGE PEEL

1 TEASPOON POWDERED LEMON PEEL

$^1/_4$ TEASPOON GROUND MACE

$^1/_2$ TEASPOON GROUND TURMERIC

$^1/_2$ TEASPOON PAPRIKA

$^1/_8$–$^1/_4$ OUNCE THYME FLOWERS

$1^1/_2$ TEASPOONS CURRY POWDER

Blend all the ingredients thoroughly, and put the resultant powder through a sieve. Store in a dry, dark place in an airtight container.

TERRE DE SIENNE

1 CUP BREAD CRUMBS

$^1/_3$–$^1/_2$ CUP PAPRIKA

$^1/_3$ CUP RAS-EL-HANOUT

1 TABLESPOON POWDERED ORANGE PEEL

2 TABLESPOONS CURRY POWDER

Blend all the ingredients thoroughly. Store the powder in a cool, dark place in an airtight container.

"TOBACCO POWDER"

1 GARLIC CLOVE

2 TABLESPOONS OIL

$^2/_3$–1 OUNCE DRIED CÈPES, GROUND TO POWDER IN A COFFEE GRINDER

Cut the garlic clove into thin strips, brown them in the oil, then dry them with paper towels.

Blend the garlic with the cèpes and put through a sieve. Store in a dry, dark place in an airtight container.

SEL CUISINÉ

3 TABLESPOONS FLEUR DE SEL

1 TABLESPOON OLIVE OIL

1 OUNCE TURNIPS, CUT IN $^1/_{16}$-INCH CUBES (BRUNOISE), PURGED WITH SALT, RINSED, AND SPONGED OFF

1 TABLESPOON ALMOND POWDER

1 BOUQUET BLANCHED BROCCOLI

1 TEASPOON CHOPPED CHIVES

PINCH OF CHOPPED TARRAGON

Mix the fleur de sel and oil. Add the turnip cubes, almond powder, blanched broccoli, chives, and tarragon and mix gently.

Sel cuisiné is a good accompaniment for grilled fish, foie gras terrines, or vegetable jellies.

NIORA PEPPER PASTE

$^1/_2$ DRIED GUINDILLA PEPPER

1 DRIED NIORA PEPPER

1 CHURIZERO PEPPER

1 SWEET RED BELL PEPPER, CHOPPED

$1^1/_2$ TABLESPOONS OLIVE OIL

1 TABLESPOON SUGAR

1 TABLESPOON SHERRY VINEGAR

1 TEASPOON TOMATO PASTE

SCANT $^1/_2$ CUP VEAL ESSENCE

Rehydrate the dried peppers in warm water. Split them in two and remove and discard the seeds. Scrape out the pulp and reserve. Soften the chopped bell pepper in the oil. Add the sugar, caramelize, and then deglaze with the vinegar.

Incorporate the tomato paste, veal essence, and reserved pepper pulp. Cook for 2 hours over very low heat. Blend, then pass the preparation through a *tamis*. Store the paste in the refrigerator in a glass container sealed with plastic wrap, or freeze in a small container.

SPICE MIXTURES AND AROMATIC PASTES

GARLIC PASTE

3 HEADS OF LAUTREC PINK GARLIC, PEELED

1¼ CUPS PEANUT OIL

½ GLASS DRY WHITE WINE

1 BAY LEAF

Blanch the garlic cloves in hot oil. When they are tender, drain them and cook them for 20–25 minutes on low heat with the white wine and bay leaf.

Remove the bay leaf and purée the garlic. Store in the refrigerator in a glass container sealed with plastic wrap.

VADOUVAN OR VANDOUVAN

10 GARLIC CLOVES

1¾ POUNDS ONIONS

1⅛ POUNDS SHALLOTS

3½ TABLESPOONS CASTOR OIL (OR MUSTARD OR PEANUT OIL)

1 TEASPOON MUSTARD SEEDS

1 TABLESPOON GROUND TURMERIC

1 TABLESPOON GROUND CUMIN

1 TEASPOON GROUND BLACK PEPPER

1 TEASPOON GROUND FENUGREEK

1 TABLESPOON SALT

1 LARGE RED, DRIED PEPPER (FAIRLY HOT)

1 TABLESPOON SHREDDED KARI (CURRY) LEAVES

Chop the garlic, onions, and shallots. Sauté in a nonstick pan with the oil, stirring constantly until perfectly caramelized and almost dried out (but don't let them burn). Add the spices, salt, red pepper, and curry leaves. Continue to toast the mixture until you have a dry brown paste. Leave to cool, and store in a glass container.

Vadouvan is the traditional spice mix of South India. It is at its best a few days after it has been made.

TOMATO MARMALADE

11 POUNDS LARGE RIPE "COEUR DE BOEUF" (BEEFHEART, OR SICILIAN) TOMATOES

1 TABLESPOON SALT

1 TABLESPOON SUGAR

1¼ CUPS VINEGAR

2 LARGE ONIONS

1⅔ CUPS OLIVE OIL

2 SPRIGS THYME

10 GARLIC CLOVES

1 BOUILLON CUBE

Chop the tomatoes in quarters and purge them for 6 hours with the salt, sugar, and vinegar.

Pour the tomatoes into a stewpot with the chopped onions, previously sautéed in the oil. Cook, covered, for 1 hour. Add a little water, along with the thyme, garlic, and stock cube, and continue cooking for another hour, uncovered, until the marmalade is thick (change the pot if the preparation caramelizes on the bottom).

Put the marmalade through a ricer or food mill; pour it into storage containers and freeze.

IT'S SMALL THINGS LIKE THIS THAT MAKE COOKING THE
DELIGHT IT IS. THIS IS A GOOD RELISH TO PREPARE IN MIDSUMMER,
THEN ENJOY FOR THE REST OF THE YEAR.

CONVERSION CHART

WEIGHT EQUIVALENTS

The metric weights given in this chart are not exact equivalents, but have been rounded up or down slightly to make measuring easier.

Avoirdupois	Metric
1/4 oz	7 g
1/2 oz	15 g
1 oz	30 g
2 oz	60 g
3 oz	90 g
4 oz	115 g
5 oz	150 g
6 oz	175 g
7 oz	200 g
8 oz (1/2 lb)	225 g
9 oz	250 g
10 oz	300 g
11 oz	325 g
12 oz	350 g
13 oz	375 g
14 oz	400 g
15 oz	425 g
16 oz (1 lb)	450 g
1 1/2 lb	750 g
2 lb	900 g
2 1/4 lb	1 kg
3 lb	1.4 kg
4 lb	1.8 kg

VOLUME EQUIVALENTS

These are not exact equivalents for American cups and spoons, but have been rounded up or down slightly to make measuring easier.

American	Metric	Imperial
1/4 tsp	1.2 ml	
1/2 tsp	2.5 ml	
1 tsp	5.0 ml	
1/2 Tbsp (1.5 tsp)	7.5 ml	
1 Tbsp (3 tsp)	15 ml	
1/4 cup (4 Tbsp)	60 ml	2 fl oz
1/3 cup (5 Tbsp)	75 ml	2.5 fl oz
1/2 cup (8 Tbsp)	125 ml	4 fl oz
2/3 cup (10 Tbsp)	150 ml	5 fl oz
3/4 cup (12 Tbsp)	175 ml	6 fl oz
1 cup (16 Tbsp)	250 ml	8 fl oz
1 1/4 cups	300 ml	10 fl oz (1/2 pint)
1 1/2 cups	350 ml	12 fl oz
2 cups (1 pint)	500 ml	16 fl oz
2 1/2 cups	625 ml	20 fl oz (1 pint)
1 quart	1 liter	32 fl oz

OVEN TEMPERATURE EQUIVALENTS

Oven Mark	F	C	Gas
Very cool	250–275	130–140	1/2–1
Cool	300	150	2
Warm	325	170	3
Moderate	350	180	4
Moderately hot	375	190	5
	400	200	6
Hot	425	220	7
	450	230	8
Very hot	475	250	9

RECIPE LIST

Published in 2007 by Stewart, Tabori & Chang
An imprint of Harry N. Abrams, Inc.

Copyright © 2006 by Éditions de La Martinière, an imprint of La Martinière
Groupe, Paris
English translation copyright © 2007 by Stewart, Tabori & Chang
Photographs copyright © 2007 by Peter Lippmann

Library of Congress Cataloging-in-Publication Data
Gagnaire, Pierre, 1950–
  Pierre Gagnaire, reinventing French cuisine / photographs by Peter
  Lippmann ; styling and recipe editing by Ric Trochon ; text by Jean-
  François Abert.
    p. cm.
  ISBN 13: 978-1-58479-657-2
  ISBN 10: 1-58479-657-X
  1. Cookery, French. 2. Menus. 3. Gagnaire, Pierre, 1950– I. Abert, Jean-
  François. II. Title.
TX719.G175 2007
641.5944—dc22
                                2007024812

Design by °Olo

Project Manager, English-language edition: Magali Veillon
Recipe Editor, English-language edition: Leah Stewart
Designer, English-language edition: Shawn Dahl
Production Manager, English-language edition: Tina Cameron

The text of this book was composed in Joanna, Profile, and Today.

Printed and bound in Singapore
10 9 8 7 6 5 4 3 2

HNA ▖▖▖▖▖
harry n. abrams, inc.
a subsidiary of La Martinière Groupe
115 West 18th Street
New York, NY 10011
www.hnabooks.com